Barbara Menzies
Malt House, H

GW00384450

THE
HEALING TOUCH

THE
HEALING TOUCH

M. H. TESTER

BARRIE & JENKINS
LONDON

First published by
Barrie & Jenkins Ltd.
2 Clement's Inn,
London, W.C.2
1970

© (Copyright) M. H. Tester 1970

SBN 257 65221 3

PRINTED IN GREAT BRITAIN
BY COX & WYMAN LTD.
LONDON, FAKENHAM AND READING

CONTENTS

LIST OF PLATES

To
Jean
whose simple faith
helped make it so.

CHAPTER ONE

I SLIPPED

THE surgical jacket that should have been saving my life was killing me. It was a monstrous piece of modern armour. The back was made of quarter-inch thick rigid polymer. It had been moulded wet to my bare skin. From the base of my neck to the top of my legs, I was held rigid. The front was made of a canvas that Navy sailmakers used to break their needles on. And the whole contraption was held impossibly tight by massive leather straps designed for medieval racks or for holding down the bonnets of vintage racing cars.

Wearing it was murder. My entire torso was encased in this contraption. Any movement was impossible. So were nearly all the small motions one needs to go through to live—like breathing. Yet if I took it off, the agony of relaxing was unbearable. My back, my right hip, the whole of my right leg and my foot were aflame with pain. I was trapped.

It all began because I did not conform to my principles. I am not a sporting man. For years I had successfully followed Oscar Wilde's advice. If I felt the need of exercise, I would lie down and make myself comfortable until the feeling passed over.

Then I decided to learn to play golf. Rack my brains as I may, I cannot remember what prompted this mad decision. Few people I knew played golf. And I felt genuinely sorry for those who did. They seemed sad, like addicts who had given up hope. Since this decision was to become the overture to events that changed my entire life, it seems strange that I cannot recall what prompted it. It could not have been chance. I now know there is no such thing. Anatole France once wrote, "Chance is the pseudonym God uses when he does not want to sign." And he was right. Suddenly, and seemingly without prompting, I was going to learn to play golf.

Although I live in Sussex, which abounds in golf courses, I was not too attracted to approaching one. There was a picture in my mind of me, on the first tee, missing drive after drive as the queue of immaculately attired and equipped scratch players got longer and longer. Nor was I enamoured by the thought of walking for hours through the long wet grass looking for the one ball I might manage to hit.

My office is in the West End of London. So I went to a nearby golf school for private lessons.

I remember it was in a lofty basement just off Wigmore Street. The instructor was a small kindly man. He put a ball on a tee on a mat. Then he hit it. He hit it, with fantastic force, straight into a net at the end of the room. Then he did it again—and once more. He seemed an ordinary sort of a fellow. It did not look too difficult.

He showed me how to do it. How to hold the club; where to place my feet; where to look; how to stand; and how to keep my head down. We tried it in slow motion. After three or four lessons I was doing fine. If there was an award for the best slow-motion golfer off Wigmore Street, I was certainly in line for it.

It was only when we speeded up the action that I met problems. I took home an old driver and a dozen practice balls. On Saturday afternoon, I carried them up to the paddock to help me solve my problem. I am the short, dark, stocky type. Although I am an Englishman, born and brought up in London and in Sussex, I can meet my ethnic counterpart anywhere on the northern shores of the Mediterranean. The key words are "short and stocky". Because when you drive off at golf you have to twist your body so that, with your feet firmly planted in the approved position, your torso starts off facing backwards and ends up facing forwards. Or some such unlikely manœuvre. This was my problem. I could not twist.

After twenty minutes' vigorous practice in the paddock, I had two more problems. I had lost all dozen practice balls, and I had acquired a prolapsed intervertebral disc between the fourth and fifth lumbar vertebrae.

Your backbone is a superb example of human engineering. It is an integrated system. It will stand enormous weights and pressures. An excessively violent shock is needed to break it. It can move in any direction supporting a weight heavier than the body of which it forms part. The full range of movements of the backbone extends from the weightlifter's clutch, through the contortions of the acrobat, to the grace and discipline of the ballet dancer.

The vertebrae are pieces of bone, each differently shaped, forming a chain from your head to your pelvis. Between each is a cushion of cartilage called a "disc". The centre of each disc is composed of a material, "nucleus pulposus", which moves about with the movement of the body. The discs act as cushions. If the backbone were solid, every step you take would jar. Discs are like shock-absorbers in a car. They also allow the backbone to move freely.

A disc can be displaced by violent or unusual movement. Sometimes the nucleus pulposus ruptures. Then the soft centre loses liquid, and this contributes to the displacement. The position of the backbone becomes distorted. The disc moves out of position and presses against the sciatic nerve—which is a great fat nerve that goes from the centre of the back down each leg. The symptoms are pain in the back and in one or sometimes both legs. The body tends to distort to compensate for the alteration of the vertebral positions.

That is what had happened to me. After a lifetime of highly organised inactivity, my backbone had lost some of its flexibility. Without warning or preparation, it was twisted through a very full range of movements. In protest, the disc in the lower back between the fourth and fifth lumbar vertebrae slipped out of position and ruptured. The soft cushion in the centre lost most of its liquid. The disc bulged on one side. The backbone slid downwards a little. The projecting part of the disc pressed against the sciatic nerve. The agony had begun.

There was an area of intense pain across the lower back. It was, in the early stages, just possible to find a position—amongst a plethora of cushions in an armchair—where the pain was tolerable. But any movement was agony. I could not stand or sit or lie down for long before the pain became torture. Yet movement made it worse. My right leg was on fire from the hip to the big toe, and no position could be found to bring any relief. My right foot was numbed with pain and I was losing all feeling on the surface of the skin. To compensate, I stood and walked in a crouching position. As a result, my right hip was about an inch and a half out of true and my right leg about two-thirds of an inch shorter than the left.

My doctor was not very surprised about it all. He called in a specialist and I was X-rayed. The results confirmed the original diagnosis. The treatment was to wear a surgical corset and to sleep flat on a board bed.

My first surgical belt was made of canvas—thick, unyielding canvas. Around it were leather-covered inserts of steel. The back was a leather pad reinforced with a steel support. The front was pulled together with saddle-leather straps.

During the day, I wore this contraption. I used a stick to get around. I tried to be brave, but I am a coward when it comes to pain. At night, I was stretched out on a board bed. Three times a day I swallowed a red capsule to kill the pain. Four times a day a black and white one was taken to make me tranquil. At night, two yellow ones were prescribed to make me sleep. My bedside table was like a pharmacy. The pills did not work very well. I was always in pain. I slept only in fits and starts and spent most of each night awake, half drugged. And I was certainly never tranquil.

With the coming of summer, the jacket became intolerably hot. Since the war, I have suffered from a neuro skin rash. The hot, sweaty canvas made this flare up. To the agony was added intense irritation. New jars of salves and more potent tranquillisers appeared at my bedside. The weather became even warmer. And so my armour was exchanged for a summer model.

This proved to be of a similar design to the original creation. For the saddle-leather at the back had been substituted chamois leather to absorb the sweat. Instead of solid canvas, there was a cotton sailcloth perforated with small holes. It was a little cooler; but there was too much give in it and, if anything, the pain became worse.

Do not imagine I was calmly accepting being a semi-cripple. I tried everything from osteopathy and manipulation to heat treatment and hanging from an iron bar. Nothing helped.

For seventeen months I endured the pain, the inconvenience, the hopelessness. I needed a holiday. We all did. In August, 1959, my wife Jean and I and the children flew to a small hotel on the coast of Brittany.

Maybe it is because of ethnic similarity or just because I learned to speak French at school that I am *sympathique* to the French. I like it in France. So do the children. They thrive on the cooking, enjoy *vin ordinaire* with their meals, and get on well with French children. The holiday at Ste. Lunaire could have been just what I needed had it not been for the beds. It was Peter Ustinov who wrote, "I can never forgive God for inventing the French." If he had written "French beds" I could have agreed with him.

They go down in the middle. No matter how you start sleeping, you end up on your side, crouching at the bottom of a steep valley. Either they do not have slipped discs in France or generations of French beds have conditioned them. But for me it was agony.

I stuck it out for five days and then consulted a doctor. French doctors seem to do everything from the other end. If you need an analgesic, they prescribe a suppository. And if you must have an injection, you get it in the bottom.

After all the undignified preliminaries, it was decided that I needed hospitalisation. Between Jean, Madame, myself and M. le Docteur we managed to convince B.E.A. that my needs were urgent. They rallied magnificently. Within an hour, I was carefully installed in the front seat of a plane at Dinard. The hostess fussed around me happily. B.E.A. hostesses must all be embryo British nannies. "No cake until you've eaten your bread and butter."

An ambulance met the plane on the tarmac at Gatwick, and half an hour later I was tucked up in a private ward in Haywards Heath Hospital. Fully sedated and out of pain for the first time for over a year, I fell asleep wondering how Jean would manage in a strange hotel with five children and the indecipherable signatures I had scribbled on my travellers' cheques.

The rack as an instrument of torture is reputed to be obsolete. This is untrue. They have one in Haywards Heath Hospital. They used it on me.

The bed was covered with a board. On this, I lay flat on my back. The foot of the bed was then raised about eighteen inches. To prevent me from sliding down on my head, a leather harness was strapped round my hips. Ropes from this were led over a pulley which was bolted to the foot of the bed. Hung on the ropes were weights. They told me the total weight was eighteen pounds, but I think they meant hundredweights.

The effect was to stretch my backbone. As I slid towards the head of the bed, the harness pulled my hips towards the foot. The vertebrae opened a little. The doctors hoped this relaxation of pressure from either side of the disc would give it room to slip back. It was an interesting experiment. They kept the traction up, day and night, for three weeks. The sheer discomfort was possibly worse than the pain, which did ease a little. They had to step up the pain-killers, the tranquillisers, the sedatives and the skin lotions.

After three weeks on the rack, the man who had made my original armour reappeared and took a wet mould of my back. From this, he made the plastic armour I was to wear when I was allowed out of bed. The specialist wanted to encase me in plaster, but by this time my skin trouble was so bad that it would have literally driven me insane. The armour could be removed to treat my skin condition. Plaster could not.

I went home thus encased—sedated, tranquillised, and hopeless —for three months convalescence.

By October, I was at the end of my tether. The pain was back in its full intensity. I could not sit, stand, lie down or assume any posture that gave me any relief. I could not drive a car, work, earn a living or have any social life. I had had enough.

I told my doctor that somewhere there must be a top authority on slipped discs. I must find that man. I must know what could be done, what I must accept, what the future held. I had to know . . .

The specialist I saw was an expert. He was the man who had written the medical textbook on slipped discs. There was no doubt that he was the last resort.

I was re-X-rayed and driven to his consulting rooms in Wimpole Street. I shuffled into his study and almost collapsed on to the examination couch. He was very thorough, very understanding, immensely knowledgeable. After I had managed to get dressed again, he delivered a concise verdict.

I had a major prolapsed disc. The displacement was gross—as large as he had seen. The pressure on the sciatic nerve of my right leg was too great to ignore. My right foot had lost almost all feeling. My only hope was for an operation to relieve the pressure. The operation would have to be performed by a neuro-surgeon since the operative site was at the junction of the spinal cord. The success factor was no higher than about forty per cent. I ought to have the operation immediately. He would like it to be done that afternoon. If I delayed too much, I might lose my leg. He could not answer for it.

I replied that I had a wife and five children, a professional practice as a surveyor, and other people to consider. I asked how long I had before an operation would be too late.

He said I had, at the most, two months.

The date was October 21st. I told him I would see him again after Christmas.

CHAPTER TWO

HOPE

So this was the end of the line. I sat in the typist's chair in my secretary's office, put my arms on her desk and buried my head in them.

The journey from Wimpole Street, although only a mile or so, had been a nightmare. The taxi driver was considerate enough. He had helped me into his cab and almost lifted me out at the other end. Between these kindly acts, he had driven as though I was an overdue mother. Or maybe he had thought I was dying, and did not want the responsibility of explaining away a warm corpse to the police. The way I was feeling, he could have been right.

My offices are on the ground floor. Which is just as well, as I had given up stairs. It was lunch time when the taxi driver deposited me. The place had been deserted except for a couple of telephone engineers trying to trace a fault in my office. If there was one thing I did not need, it was company. I had shuffled into my secretary's room. She was out, too. So I sat at her desk and brooded on what the specialist had said.

I do not like hospitals. I like surgical operations even less. The thought of a neuro-surgeon opening up my lower back and trying to reach the slipped disc through the tangled mass of knitting that was my central nervous system was horrific. The prospect of a few weeks in a hospital bed was bad enough. To spend this time on my face seemed too high a price. Then I remembered the throwaway line the specialist had used when he mentioned the low success factor of this operation. He preferred to use a neuro-surgeon because, in this operational site, a mistake could result in paralysis.

My secretary kept a carafe of water in her room. I poured a glass and washed down a pain-killer and a tranquilliser. Then, in the brief period when the pain level dropped a little and before I became dozy, I did my thinking.

There were two simple courses of action open to me. The first was to accept the expensive and specialised advice I had been given. If the operation succeeded, I should be free of pain but I would probably have a weak back for the rest of my life. Getting the centre of a prolapsed disc back again is like getting the tooth-paste back into the tube. It won't go. The operation mainly consists of cutting off the section of the disc that is protruding. The cushioning effect is, of course, lessened for ever. The operation could be unsuccessful. In which case, I would be no better off and considerably weaker. There could be further complications and a nerve might accidentally be severed or damaged. Some degree of paralysis might result.

The second course was to do nothing. This meant that the pain, the discomfort, and the physical and social restrictions would continue. And I could jeopardise my right leg if the pressure be-came too great. I was attached to that leg. Thank God, I still am.

I had come to the end of the road. Before me it forked. One way led to the life of a semi-cripple—to pain and discomfort, to the possibility of losing a leg. That did not seem the way. The other path led to hospital—to an operation, to discomfort and to some risk of permanent paralysis. That did not seem the way, either. I put my head in my arms again. I was stuck.

A leading psychiatrist once told me that the most commanding sound in the world is the cry of a baby. He said that in pitch, volume and modulation it was designed always to command atten-tion. He forgot the telephone. This one was very demanding. Emo-tionally drained and slightly tranquillised, I looked at it as if from a great distance. Here was a simple problem. Here, also, were two possible solutions. Either somebody answered it or the caller would become tired and hang up. I had examined the problem, pronounced my judgment and confidently waited for one of the alternatives to take place. Tester, the decision-maker. Solomon must have felt like this.

Somewhere at the back of my mind there was born a small doubt. And it grew. No one answered the phone. The caller did not hang up. The phone kept on ringing. Maybe there was another alternative. Maybe there always is . . . I picked up the telephone.

There is a saying, "Saved by the bell". It will always hold a special meaning for me.

By profession I am a surveyor—a consultant on shop property. The man on the telephone was a property man. You could call him a client since I had done some minor jobs for him. That he was wealthy and successful I did know. It must have been two or three months since I had last spoken to him. His call was not important. We spoke for a few minutes on professional and business matters. My tone, or perhaps my manner, must have been a little strange, for he said, "You sound depressed. Tell me what is troubling you."

The confessional box and the analyst's couch owe their continued popularity to the relief that off-loading one's troubles always brings. It is a form of mental catharsis. There I was, loaded with trouble. And there he was, ready to listen. So I told him the whole story.

I do not know what reaction I expected. The usual one used to be to recommend me to a manipulator who worked wonders for old so-and-so, or to swear by Nurse Oddbody's Old-Fashioned Back Liniment, or to suggest a long holiday. From him, I got none of these. No pity, and not much sympathy. Instead, in a brisk and businesslike voice, he asked me, "If I send you to somebody who could help you, will you go without asking silly questions?" Would I? I would go anywhere, see anybody. The mere suggestion that there was a third fork in the road would send me haring off to find it. "I'll ring you back," he said.

Less than fifteen minutes later, he was on the phone again. He had made an appointment for me to see a Mr. Edward Fricker at five-thirty that evening at 40 Howard Road in the London suburb of South Tottenham.

The third road was signposted.

CHAPTER THREE

HELP AND HEALING?

LONDON is my home-town. Although I live in Sussex, I was born in London and went to school there. I was a student in Lincoln's Inn Fields and an articled pupil in Baker Street. I grew up, sowed my wild oats and met my wife in London. My offices are in the West End, but I know the whole sprawling city and can take you through the back-doubles of Battersea as easily as I can through Mayfair. But South Tottenham . . .

There are those who claim we now live in a classless society. So if I talk of the working class or the middle class they pretend not to understand. But Londoners know. They even have sub-divisions like "lower middle class". Tottenham is lower middle class. It is an area with some coherency. It boasts a world-famous football team, a busy shopping centre and a zest for life. When Thoreau wrote "It is life near the bone, where it is sweetest", he could have been thinking of Tottenham.

A mile or so away is Stoke Newington. Once an upper middle class suburb of the city, it has now come down in the world. Most of the houses have been demolished. In their place, the local council have built great slab blocks of flats. For the life of me I can never understand the philosophy behind this planning. A street of houses has character. Each house is a cell in a community: the cell in which the smallest unity of communal life thrives and functions—the family.

In the Victorian era, hundreds of small terrace houses were built speculatively. In a street, the odd numbers were on one side and the even numbers were on the other. They were the only distinguishing features except for small variations in the net curtains. You approached each house by opening an identical wrought-iron gate set in a cement-capped dwarf brick wall. The "front garden" was a paved area six feet deep. The front elevation was of yellow London stock brickwork relieved by cement rendering on the lintels and sills. A small bay window, on the ground floor only, had the flat front and the sloping sides of a six-sided figure sliced in half. Up a well-whitened front step and you were in the hall.

On one side of the hall a straight-up staircase rose to the only upper floor. If the staircase was on your left, you would find the entrance to the front parlour on your right. It was not a sitting room, or a drawing room, or a lounge. It was a front parlour. The curtains were heavy and managed, with added net appendages, to cut out most of the light. The furniture included an upright piano, two armchairs and a sofa. The floor was carpeted. A hanging light-fitting held four imitation electric candles with shades. And the atmosphere of eternal preservation, furniture polish and still air was only disturbed for four functions: births, weddings, funerals and courting.

Behind the parlour was the dining room. It was practically filled by a large table, six or eight chairs, a couple of fireside chairs, a television set, and a contraption of cupboards, drawers and shelves that was a cross between a Dutch dresser and a Greek-Orthodox hearse. This was the sideboard.

Upstairs were one large, one small and one diminutive bedroom, and a bathroom.

At the rear of the house was the "back addition"—a slate-roofed single-storey example of jerry-building—occupying only half the plot width and housing the kitchen, an outside water closet and a small solid fuel boiler and coal store.

Beyond was a small piece of waste ground, enclosed by rotting fencing, known as "the garden". Sometimes you would find there a minute shed where a man pursued his hobby, kept pigeons, or hid the brown ale. There would be two home-made wire-fronted hutches for the guinea-pigs or rabbits, and a kennel for the dog.

Each house looked like its neighbour. It *was* like its neighbour. But to the occupants, each was unique. It was the place where they were born, became engaged, married, conceived and cele-brated the births of their children. And they knew their relations would gather one day in the front parlour, in their best clothes, to go through the barbaric rituals that their death demanded.

The planners took streets of these living vibrant cells and demolished them. In their place, they erected monstrous blocks of flats. Like letters in a massive bank of pigeon-holes, the families were slotted in.

Now, they are high above the streets where once they played. They have no garden, no dog, no shed, no guinea-pigs, no rabbits. The isolation, the height, the feeling of being forgotten, the impersonal life in a box after the zest and bustle of a street is all too much. Family life withers and dies. The children grow up and drift away. And the breakdown of the family as the primary unit in community life is a main cause of crime and immorality. If this is planning—give me chaos . . .

Between Tottenham and Stoke Newington is a sprawling mass of these little terrace houses. They wait patiently for the bulldozers to arrive. Until then, the children play in the streets, the dogs chase one another, the motorbike leans against the front wall as the leather-jacketed Romeo chats-up his Cockney Juliet, the Monday wash flutters in the gardens, and no man's underwear is a secret from his neighbours. And the street lives.

Howard Road is just such a street. The taxi driver knew where it was. He was probably born around the corner. He half-lifted me out of his cab and deposited me like a precious antique at the front gate of No. 40. As he drove off, I looked at this small house. It was unlike its neighbours in one particular. By the front door was a well-polished brass plate. On it were engraved the enigmatic words FRICKER'S HEALING CENTRE.

The door was closed. I pressed the bell-push. While I waited, I thought about doors: the ones I had gone through to pain, to discomfort and to disillusionment; the ones that had remained closed. It seemed a long way away, but only that morning I had stood at the door of the specialist in Wimpole Street to be admitted to a verdict I was loath to accept. They had carried me through the door of the ambulance and wheeled me through the door of the hospital ward. The cab driver had manhandled me through the door of the taxi. And here I was, like a mouldering relic encased in plastic, held together with straps, propped up with a stick.

Doors. Had not the man said, "Ask and it shall be given to you; seek and ye shall find; knock and it shall be opened unto you"? I knocked. The door opened.

I do not know what I had expected—a nurse in a little cap; an angel with shimmering wings; an enormous man with strong thumbs and a white coat . . . She was young and pretty. She wore a twin-set and a tweed skirt. I gave my name and she asked me in.

No. 40 Howard Road proved to be not at all the same as its neighbours. To begin with, it was full of people. The hall was crowded. I followed the girl through a packed mass like a rush-hour on the Piccadilly tube. We found ourselves crushed against the dining room door. She managed to find the handle and we were in. But there was no dining room.

The partition wall between the front parlour and the rear dining room had been taken away. There was just one large room. In the bay window was a cheap wooden desk, at which my little guide seated herself importantly. She turned to an obsolete typewriter and started striking the keys as if they needed disciplining.

In the centre of the room was a low table covered with elderly coverless magazines. Linoleum and a couple of druggets hid the floor. Against the walls were kitchen chairs. They were all occupied.

Do you remember The Courtship of the Yonghy-Bonghy-Bo?

> Two old chairs, and half a candle —
> One old jug without a handle —
> These were all his worldly goods.

Lear's silly lines kept running round my head. I wanted to giggle. The atmosphere was right, and the chairs certainly were. Why do they call them kitchen chairs? Go into any kitchen today and you find either no chairs at all or some of those stainless-steel tube and plastic upholstery abortions they call "modern". But these have surely never seen a kitchen. They have round seats with a design burnt into them incorporating small drilled holes. Ventilation for hot bottoms, I suppose. The legs are wooden and round. The backs are upright, with a rounded top. Once, they were stained dark brown. Wear and tear and the passage of many posteriors have worn them down to the bare wood in places. They were packed together, each touching the one on either side. Every inch of wall space was filled. Every chair was occupied.

Cervantes, in *Don Quixote*, wrote: "Tell me thy company and I will tell thee what thou art." I was sick; in pain; at the end of my tether—but buoyed up by the hope that there must be something else. Suffering leaves an imprint. So does hope. The company was deeply marked with these two impressions. I was among my fellows.

Englishmen do not stare. I leaned against the door, which was the only clear space in the room, and looked politely around. They were all looking politely at me. Then a bell pinged and a door at the far end of the room opened. There was a mutter of voices in the hall. A sigh passed through the waiting company. They shifted their positions. One woman got up, straightened her skirt, smiled at her neighbour and walked through the far door, which closed behind her. I moved across the room and sat in the vacated chair.

The centre door opened and a man came in from the hall, glanced at those waiting, leaned against the door and started reading the newspaper he held. Our number was again complete.

They were a mixed bunch. On my left was a bus conductor. You know my methods, Watson: the worn skin of the right forefinger from pressing the bell; the mark on the left hip where he leans against the seats; the ink on the fingers from the ticket machine. My powers of observation are not that precise. There was another indication: he was wearing a bus conductor's uniform. He had asthma and experienced some trouble in breathing. On the other side of me was a middle-aged blonde with a Louis XIV hairstyle and crutches. Opposite, a woman held on firmly to a small child with a withered arm. A well-dressed Negro sat like a stoic turned inward on his suffering. Two labourers in soiled jeans and thick boots whispered together behind the *Evening Standard*. A neat, trim brunette with superb legs kept her head turned lest we should look too closely at the disfiguring sores on her cheek. An old man coughed into a large red handkerchief. A child whimpered. They sat there—every one of them ill, yet all with the aura of hope.

The walls were covered with newspaper cuttings in passe-partout frames. Some were old and yellow. Many were cut from local papers— *The Hackney Gazette, The South Western Star*. Several were from *Two Worlds*, which sounded like space-fiction. All told of amazing cures, dumbfounded doctors, surprised specialists. One theme was common to them all: "Fricker heals again." It was permutated in varying headlines. CRIPPLE WALKS AFTER 12 YEARS; DEAF MAN HEARS; I HAVE THROWN AWAY MY CRUTCHES says patient; AMAZING CURE BAFFLES DOCTORS; HEALING HANDS; CAN HE WORK MIRACLES?

Can he work miracles?

There was a murmur of voices in the hall. A rustle disturbed the waiting company. The bell pinged and the far door opened. The little girl in the twin-set and tweed skirt stood before me. "Mr. Fricker will see you now."

I was going to find out.

CHAPTER FOUR

THE "MIRACLE"

At school, I was taught classics. The two most important subjects were Greek and Latin. At the time, I thought them both part of an obsolete educational tyranny. Now I am not so sure. The Greek lessons gave me an agile mind and an appreciation of fine living. The Latin lessons taught me the basis of many European languages and opened the doors to pre-Christian philosophy.

I knew nothing of the man called Fricker. On the brass plate it said FRICKER'S HEALING CENTRE. Was he a faith healer? What could he do where doctors and specialists had failed? Yet from the forgotten depths of somewhere, a Latin tag appeared in my mind. I think it was Tertullian, but I cannot be sure. It was so long ago. Then why should I suddenly remember so very clearly those few words of schoolboy Latin? "Certum est quia impossibile est." And the simple translation: "It is certain because it is impossible."

Edward George Fricker—whom everybody called either "Mr. Fricker" or just "Ted"—turned out to be a middle-aged, plump, jolly Cockney in shirtsleeves. He took my hand warmly as I shuffled into the little room that had been converted out of the back-addition kitchen. The gold-rimmed spectacles sparkled as he brightly enquired after Tony (the businessman whose telephone call had started me on this strange journey).

The room was small. A thick carpet covered the floor. In one corner was a basin of water, a towel and the aroma of Zolflora Carnation, a popular disinfectant. The only items of furniture were an armchair, two low stools and a radiogram, on top of which sat a wooden salad bowl filled with ten-shilling notes, pound notes, fivers and silver. On the walls were an odd collection of indifferently executed religious paintings. About the room were an assortment of sacred emblems. A crucifix rubbed shoulders with a Buddha, a Star of David with a rosary.

The tubby little man, his bulging waistcoat complete with gold watch-chain, beamed happily at me, sat me on the larger of the two stools and asked me what was wrong. I told him. The thought of the patiently-waiting multitude gave wings to my tongue. I kept the story short, to the point, and purely factual. He listened without interruption. His only remark was to ask me to take my coat off.

"Are you a faith healer?" I asked.

"Not exactly," he replied.

"Do I need to have faith in you?"

"I don't care whether you have faith or not. I have all the faith that is necessary."

At his request, I stood up. He put his left hand on my stomach and ran his right hand lightly up and down my backbone. He soon located the disc that was the cause of all the trouble. I was wearing the thick polythene orthopaedic jacket, but through this he had located the precise area of the lesion. He would have needed a power-drill to reach my skin.

He asked me to remove the spinal jacket, and I had to get him to help me out of it. When I was back to my shirt and trousers again, he started the same manœuvre. His left hand remained on my stomach. The right hand rubbed across the lumbar region and up and down the backbone. There was no manipulation. The pressure was no more than that you would apply in stroking a cat. He extended the area to include my much distorted right hip.

How long this went on, I cannot say. I was in a funny state of mind. Hope of a miracle cure was being reorientated by the complete simplicity of the "treatment". All he was doing was rubbing my back with as little emphasis as a mother's "there-there" soothing of a hurt child. Afterwards, I realised I could not have been with him for more than ten minutes. I subsequently learned that patients seldom exceeded this time. And some waited hours to be with him for even less.

Now I can clearly see that this moment was the turning point in my life. At the time, I felt little except a real lessening of the pain and a feeling of bewilderment. After nearly two years of agony, frustration and discomfort I felt the first wave of natural, relaxed relief. And all this because a tubby Cockney had spent a few minutes rubbing his hand up and down my back. I was determined to say nothing—to accept any blessings and try to work it out later.

Fricker went out of the room and came back with a sheet of brown paper. Humming happily, he made an untidy parcel of my spinal jacket and handed it to me, beaming. "Take that home under your arm," he said. "Throw that stick away. Take the board out of your bed and sleep normally on the mattress. And come and see me next week."

As I walked dazedly out, I heard the ping of the bell. Before I had taken two paces, the next patient was being greeted by this extraordinary man. What was he? A miracle-every-ten-minutes man?

You will note that I wrote "walked": because I was walking, not shuffling. I still had some pain in my right leg, but it was much lessened. My back was still aching, but only slightly. My right hip was still distorted. But I could walk.

With my head high and with a firm step I walked out through the front door, my untidy parcel and my stick under my arm. Something wonderful had happened.

One of the dangers of a conventional education is that you might learn to think conventionally. Miracles have happened. They can be recognised because an angel comes down from heaven; or there is a burning bush, a change of light, and the strains of unearthly music. We talk of "the miracle of Dunkirk". What about the miracle of German organisation and planning that made the withdrawal necessary? We call an earthquake an act of God. Why is not a sunset, or a perfect snowflake, or the mathematics of astro-navigation an act of God? Are miracles things that only happened to people hundreds of years ago? Do you need a long-haired, bearded gentleman in a white nightgown to do them? Can one be done by a tubby Cockney in his shirtsleeves? I remember Emerson's comforting remark in his *Method of Nature* that when Nature has work to be done she creates a genius to do it. Was Ted Fricker a genius?

There were no taxis in Howard Road. The little girl in the

twin-set had taken the improvement in my walk and posture as an
everyday occurrence. It probably was, to her. She gave me an
appointment for the following week and telephoned for a hire-car.
The driver was used to these trips. He had driven many sick
people from Fricker's Healing Centre. He did not seem very
surprised at my experience. "It happens all the time," he said.

The small car negotiated the heavy evening traffic between
South Tottenham and Victoria. It bumped over uneven roads,
braked, turned, stopped and started as the driver went through
the traditional gyrations of the London motorist. I did not feel a
thing. I still had an ache in my leg and my back felt a little sore,
but there was no real pain. And the movements of the car did not
induce any. An hour before, every slight change of direction of the
taxi had been agonising.

The drive to Victoria took half an hour. My thoughts, like Don
Quixote's, ran a-wool-gathering. One thing I did know. I was
much much better. And I made two resolutions I knew I had to
keep. Whatever happened, I would see this thing through; and
then I would find out what really had been done to me.

British Railways, Southern Region, have now introduced move-
able head-rests and adjustable seats on some trains. But at this
time they were yet to come. I had developed a hatred of their
seats. There was insufficient support for my back, and the distance
from the back to the front of the seat cushion was much too long.
Whatever posture I adopted, I could not avoid acute discomfort.
And whenever the driver rattled over points or jerked the carriages
up and down the train like beads on a string, which he did very
often, I was in pain.

That night the seats were soft, comfortable and exquisitely
designed. The driver was an accomplished artist, handling the long
train with a feather-light touch. There were no points, and the
rubber wheels ran smoothly over the thickly carpeted rails.

Jean collected me at the station. Her face was alight with
wonder and feminine curiosity as she saw the brown-paper parcel
and the stick under my arm, and noted the ease with which
I walked and got into her car. I kissed her cheek but was too
overcome to talk. "Take me home," I said, "and I'll tell you all
about it."

The Droveway House is a large, comfortable house with a

thatched roof, a small lake, a swimming-pool and about six acres of most attractive grounds. Yet it is under a mile from Haywards Heath Station.

We used to live in the centre of London—in Harley House, which backs on to Regent's Park. It was a convenient place to live, with the West End before you and the park behind. We had a summer place at Selsey Bill in Sussex by the sea. Every weekend in the summer saw us driving down on Friday night and home again on Sunday evening. We have five children now, but in those days there were only three. As the kids got bigger, the car more crowded and the traffic thicker, we decided to move out of central London and combine both homes in one.

Commuting is seldom a pleasure, but I reckoned I could drive, say, ten miles to the office. So we drew a circle of ten-mile radius on the road-map, with Mayfair as the centre. Then, one Sunday, we drove round the circumference. It was pure suburbia.

We increased the radius to twelve miles, then to fifteen and eventually to twenty miles. Still suburbia. All we found were rows and rows of identical houses, concrete roads, uniformity and regimented dullness.

It looked like an impasse. I could not envisage driving over twenty miles to my office. It would mean travelling forty miles a day. Then Jean suggested the trains. "Let's move right away from London," she reasoned. "Right into the country—into Sussex."

I telephoned Southern Region Information. "What place in Sussex," I asked, "has the best train service to London?"

They told me without hesitation. "Haywards Heath—nearly one hundred trains a day each way, and many running non-stop in forty-six minutes."

"Right," I said to Jean, a master of decision. "I'm very busy. *You* go to Haywards Heath and buy a house."

Two nights later, over dinner, I said to Jean, "What did you do today, darling?" Every husband says this. He is seldom curious. There he is, grappling with the complex problems of survival— and all she has to do is flick a feather duster about, order a few delicacies, and make no decisions more important than whether she should use Pink Panther or Scarlet Sighs on her fingernails.

"I went to Haywards Heath," she replied, all wide-eyed and innocent.

Now she had my attention. "Did you buy a house?" I enquired from my height of manly property know-how.

"Yes." And taking a deep breath, "It's only a mile from the station, with an enormous thatched roof, eight or nine bedrooms, six or seven acres of gardens, and a lake, and it's just what we always wanted and I said we would have it and that you would drive down with me on Saturday morning and clinch the deal."

We drove down on Saturday. Once you get out of London and through Surrey, you come to Sussex. This is Tester country, and I love the leafy lanes, the open downland, the smell and the sight of it. We came upon The Droveway House up a long drive between massed ranks of silver birches. It was as Jean had described it—a piece of pure Sussex. As we walked through the house and by the little lake, I remembered:

> Peace and rest at length have come,
> All the day's long toil is past;
> And each heart is whispering, Home
> Home at last!

This was home.

We had no money. I did not think I could raise the ten-per-cent deposit and the price seemed astronomical. But this was home. We had to have it. So we did.

Today, The Droveway House is a show place. The gardens, under the design of Jean and the work of our gardener and friend James Ellis, are a joy of colour and rest. We have re-thatched the roof, modernised the bathrooms and the kitchen, put in central heating, laid out formal gardens, built a swimming-pool, planted more trees, added more wings, and built new garaging. But basically it is as we saw it that Saturday—home.

And here I was in my home, sitting down to an evening meal and, between mouthfuls, telling Jean all about my wonderful experience.

After supper, we took the board out of the bed. It stood there against the foot of the bed, a reminder of hundreds of tortured nights.

"Shall we keep it? No—let's burn it! "

CHAPTER FIVE

WHEN YOU CLOSE YOUR EYES,
IT DOESN'T GO AWAY

HAVE you ever had something happen to you so wonderful, so exciting, so unusual that you would not tell anybody about it in case it disappeared or seemed less? That is how I felt. Something wonderful had happened to me. Although I still had a few bearable aches and pains, my body felt better than it had for years. It was light, free of tension, relaxed and flexible. I was sleeping well and had stopped taking all those coloured capsules. The board from the bed had been ceremoniously burned. The surgical jacket was put away. My stick stayed in the hallstand. Sciatica in my right leg still troubled me. My hip was still out of true. But I was upright and walking. And I felt altogether different.

When I was in my late teens, I forsook orthodox religion. The rituals, superstitions, folklore and threats that made up the belief in which I was raised seem sterile and stupid. Over the years, I had sought spiritual truth. I had prayed in synagogues and listened to rabbis. I had sat through almost every variation of Christian service, from the simplicity of the Unitarians to the complexity of full Catholic Mass. I had argued with Jesuits, Buddhist monks, Seventh Day Adventists, maharishis and the custodians of mosques. My personal research into comparative religions had led me to read every holy book I could lay my hands on. I read the Old and the New Testaments in half a dozen versions. I studied the sacred books of India—both Hindu and Moslem—the Koran and the Talmud. The Chinese fascinated me at one time, and I must have read every book in my local library on Confucius and Taoism. Back in history, I came upon Mithras and Baal and the now forgotten but strangely familiar gods of the ancient Egyptians.

Running through them all I could recognise the golden thread of truth woven into a pure philosophy. But everywhere it was distorted, overlaid, camouflaged and changed by the growth of an orthodoxy. The more I studied the bare bones of religions the more I became impressed not by the differences but by the similarities. I was suffering from a spiritual hunger. I needed to knock and have a door opened to me.

Most of us need two things. The first is to have a simple but utterly convincing demonstration of psychic power. The second is to understand the spiritual implications. In a confused way, I now felt these needs. Maybe—and only maybe—Ted Fricker had shown me the power of healing. Maybe I was on the threshold of the breakthrough I had sought for years. Maybe.

I was excited. I felt I was in front of a door I had been seeking all my life. I would go on knocking. But for the present, I would tell no one. Jean promised, too, to keep silent—a hard restriction.

Twice more I visited the little house in Howard Road. Each visit was like the last. The hallway was crowded, the waiting room full. Some of the patiently waiting people I recognised. Some were strangers.

There is a certain apathy in a doctor's waiting room. The patients are there with chronic ailments or incurable minor maladies, or to get a certificate or an injection. None expects to emerge with bounding hope. Johnson's question of Boswell "Are you sick or are you sullen?" could have been written in a doctor's waiting room. The patients are sick. They are sullen, too—with the sullenness that goes with lack of hope.

This waiting room was different. These maladies, I could recognise, were major ones. The men, women and children seated uncomplaining on those hard kitchen chairs showed the deformities, the weaknesses and the general symptoms of the medically incurable. As I got to know the room better, I learned to recognise the steel braces of polio, the crutches of the dislocated vertebrae, the wheeze of asthma and the shuffle of the arthritic. Some kept to themselves; others proudly displayed their maladies and discussed them with their neighbours. Many sat in silence and bore "the insupportable labour of doing nothing".

Once, I came in the morning. Another time, in the afternoon. There was no difference. Every few minutes the bell pinged, a patient left, another slipped through the door at the rear and one more came in from the hall. We all shifted our buttocks, nursed our symptoms, coughed and waited on.

Each time, when it was my turn to go through the door, the routine was the same. I took off my coat and sat on a stool, or stood facing the tiled mantelpiece with its odd collection of religious bric-à-brac. Fricker sometimes played a record on the radiogram. I could never recognise the music, but it sounded like something from a musical comedy. His right hand did the work, rubbing lightly up and down my back or tracing the line of the sciatic nerve down my right leg. His left hand rested on my shoulder or my stomach. He would ask me how I was. Otherwise, there was minimal conversation. After a few minutes, he turned off the music, helped me on with my coat and told me to come again next week. He always worked in his shirtsleeves, seemed confident and happy, and never took more than ten minutes from the time I entered his room until I left it.

The improvement in my condition was marked and progressive. Railway seats had lost their horrors and I was commuting again to the office. Everything in the garden was lovely. Until a couple of days after my third visit.

Then, suddenly, it was back—the whole complex pattern spelling out the syndrome of agony.

I am a coward. Physical pain is my idea of hell. People have different threshold levels of pain. Mine is not very high. I hurt easily and I react quickly. Jean, now, is quite different. She can stand pain and relegate it to the back of her mind. Many women can. I have no idea who wrote "Man endures pain as an undeserved punishment, woman accepts it as a natural heritage." But he was a pretty acute observer of human behaviour.

On top of the physical pain, I had what Scott called "The sickening pang of hope deferred"—a nice description of how I felt, even if he did lift it from the Book of Proverbs. The healing I had received was changing both my body and my philosophy. Suddenly, I was back where I started—my right leg aflame with pain, my back stiff and aching.

On the Monday, I was too ill to go to the office. I sat propped in an armchair in the sitting room, brooding on my misfortune and reading. And there it was. Written by a woman who had been blind and deaf from childhood, cut off from her fellows. Denied the very elements of communication, Helen Keller had written, "Keep your face to the sunshine and you cannot see the shadow." Away with pity. Tomorrow I would get to Ted Fricker, even if I had to be carried. I was determined to be healed.

Next day, I painfully edged myself into the passenger seat of Jean's Sheerline and tried to concentrate sufficiently to navigate her from East Sussex to South Tottenham. It is a tiring journey through suburban Surrey and the sprawl of outer London and it took Jean over two and a half hours, driving with great care. Every bump was agony for me; every sway had its own painful memory. It seemed like two and a half weeks.

CHAPTER SIX

A DOOR OPENS

TED FRICKER was like a man possessed—which he probably was. The music poured from the record-player. His right hand positively vibrated over my back and leg. As the music became louder, he built up into a crescendo of vibrating movement. Then it was silent. He stopped, washed his hands and said, "You'll be all right now. Come again next week."

On the way home, the traffic was heavier. The journey took three hours. We were both tired and hungry. But nothing mattered. The intense pain had gone. The few residual aches were forgotten in the glorious thanksgiving of being healed. We were on our way.

On that journey, I mused at the strange power that flowed through Fricker's hands. It was not faith healing. I had gone to him with no knowledge of what he could do, or of his reputation. I had no faith. He did not talk very much and had not even attempted to induce an emotional response. The atmosphere was prosaic. The religious symbols and paintings were of poor workmanship. The music was indifferent. Certainly there was no emotional response on my part. And even if there had been, could it correct the severe orthopaedic condition I suffered?

That the healing came from a source outside the healer I felt convinced. The words of the Apocrypha, "For of the most High cometh healing"—could they apply? Yet what sort of a vehicle had He chosen?

Torn between the desire to accept my blessing without question and an innate thirst for knowledge, I argued with Jean all the way home. We reached no conclusion. I had consulted the best doctors, the most learned specialists. They had been able to do nothing to heal my infirmity. Their only success had been to slightly ameliorate the symptoms. A last-hope major operation was the only remaining course untried. Nearly two years of crippling pain, acute discomfort and complete social and professional paralysis had been terminated not by a physician but by a tubby Cockney with no medical qualifications, almost no conversation, and a technique any medical school would revile. Yet I was better. Much better.

I called on Fricker a total of six or seven times, at intervals of seven or eight days. Each "treatment" was much the same. We rarely spoke except to exchange pleasantries and for me to report progress.

By the middle of November, I had resumed my normal, professional life. Every day, I journeyed the forty-odd miles to the office by train and car. Every evening, I travelled home again. Apart from an odd twinge along the sciatic nerve and a spasmodic ache or two in my back, I was well. The family doctor, who made a routine call, was amazed to see me trotting around happily and even dancing a few carefree steps to a new LP.

I was going to write that the doctor was "surprised". But I remembered Johnson, who had an unusual command of the English language. He was caught one day kissing the maid. His wife, who found him thus, said, "Well, Sam, I am surprised!" To which the witty doctor replied, "No, my dear, *you* are amazed. It is I who am surprised." So my doctor was truly amazed.

He made me walk up and down, sit down and get up, and generally gyrate before him. Not only was I upright where I had been bent, mobile where I had been fixed and happy where I had been miserable, but my hip was now only very slightly larger than its fellow. And my two legs were the same length. I had discarded the built-up shoe, the spinal jacket, the stick.

I was subjected to a vigorous examination, and there was no doubt as to the verdict. I was healed.

There is always tea on the go at The Droveway House. Jean drinks gallons, and the large china mugs seem to be in constant demand by James Ellis and his odd-job helpers in the garden as well as by Taffy the milkman, the window cleaners, any visiting delivery boy, the postmen and the dustmen; to say nothing of the school holidays, when our five children invite everybody's children in for tea. So we gave the doctor some.

Between us, Jean and I told him the whole story. His face was alight with interest although, alas, we could answer none of his questions as to how or why. But we were determined to find out.

Since then, we have had the Frug, the Hitch-hiker, the Locomotion and La Bamba: but that year was the year of the Twist. I am unsure where it started, but it swept America, crossed the Atlantic and took over Europe. *Le twist* was "in".

You stood facing your partner. The music was an eight-to-the-bar off-beat. You moved your feet to left or right, held your elbows well in and twisted your pelvis in time to that fast tempo. What it did to backbones I hesitate to think. Old people, or anyone too rigid, could not do it. The youngsters loved it. The experienced Twister could keep his shoulders level and yet twist his hips through a wide arc. Watching a room full of dancers made me think it had been invented by an orthopaedic surgeon in need of patients.

That Christmas, I did the Twist. Maybe it was not up to the gyrating standards of the teenagers but it was the Twist, or a reasonable facsimile. I twisted with enjoyment, relaxed and happy. I was healed. And I was eternally grateful for it.

I was healed. My back was straight. My right hip was still fractionally larger than my left—but you would need an accurate measurement to appreciate it. My right leg was now as long as my left. I was free of pain, relaxed and happy.

You cannot just walk in on a specialist. There is a proper procedure that you must follow. So I went back to my doctor, who was still amazed at my good health, and asked him to make an appointment with the orthopaedic physician I had seen two months earlier.

The taxi pulled up at the smart door in Wimpole Street. I leapt out, paid the fare, added a large tip and happily mounted the front steps.

The specialist had on his desk my medical file, the X-rays and his original diagnosis. "You wanted to see me after Christmas," I said, "so here I am. Please examine me."

The examination took over half an hour. It was as thorough as the previous one. He tested every muscle in my back and legs, and tried every reflex. Each time he moved a joint, he asked, "Does that

hurt?" Each time he got a negative answer. The man was getting
very puzzled. My leg movement at knee and hip was free and
normal. My complete flexibility at the back was demonstrated as I
touched my toes and straightened up without effort. At three stages
in the examination, he consulted the file—once to read his previous
notes and twice to look closely at the X-rays. "Something has been
done to you. What is it?" he asked. But I would not tell him—at
least, not then. At my insistence, he completed the examination
and delivered his verdict.

"You are almost completely cured," he admitted at last. "You
have all the characteristics of a man successfully cured of a slipped
disc. Within four to six weeks, I would expect the remaining symptoms to clear up. There is a poor muscle tone in those parts of the
leg you have not used much. This will improve. You may get odd
sciatic twinges over a period as long as six months. These will
lessen and disappear. Congratulations. No further treatment is
necessary and certainly no operation is now needed. Now, tell me
how it was done." But I would not. There were two more questions
I needed to put.

I asked him if it was possible that I could have been made better
by a natural and spontaneous process. If there was any possibility
that a slipped disc of this seriousness could have corrected itself
on its own, this man should know. After all, I was in the presence
of the top expert in this field. His reply left no room for doubt.
He emphasised it by vigorously shaking his head. "There was, in
your case, no possibility of natural remission—none at all."

There remained one alternative. "Is there any possibility that
what was wrong with me was psychosomatic?" I asked. We hear a
lot these days of emotionally induced illness. Many complaints are
classified in medical clinics with the letters E.I.I. If there was any
possibility that my illness could have been one for which my mind
was responsible, this seemed important. But he was just as em-
phatic. He pointed to the X-rays, to the doctor's report, to the local
orthopaedic surgeon's diagnosis and to the results of his own
meticulous tests. "No. Out of the question," was his positive
answer.

So I told him about my visit to Fricker the very evening after
my first consultation. I told him about the "treatments" I had
received and how I had taken off my spinal jacket never to wear it

again. He listened without interruption to the tale of the bed-board we had burned, the stick I no longer used, the change that had taken place in my basic frame, and the resumption of my full professional and social life. His amazement deepened when I capped it all with my recollection of how I danced the Twist at Christmas.

He had no words. What I had told him cut across a lifetime of medical experience. He was baffled and could offer no explanation.

My doctor holds two letters. They are both from this same specialist. The first, written after my initial examination in October, confirms the diagnosis and recommends an immediate operation. The second, written in January, says merely that I am well and no further action is necessary.

He was not the only man who was baffled. I was, too. Perhaps I had seen a glimmer of light. The healing I had received did not feel strange or unreal. It was a natural and acceptable thing. My long illness and the strange way I had been directed to that little house in Howard Road had the semblance of a pattern. At the back of my mind was a remark made, I think, by Aughey: "God brings men into deep waters, not to drown them but to cleanse them." That I had been in deep waters there was no doubt. Had I been cleansed? The only way to find out was to ask.

I went to see Fricker again.

Healers have always existed. Jesus was a healer; so was Moses. The ancient Egyptians had healer priests. In almost every race, at almost any time, healing was practised. It is mentioned often in the holy books of all the great religions of the world. I reminded myself that in Ecclesiasticus it says "For of the most High cometh healing", which suggests healing comes from God. I decided to ask Fricker.

He was pleased to see me, but not surprised that I was so completely well. He said it happened all the time. He had lost count of the thousands (thousands?) of slipped discs he had healed. He knew the healing came from God. He heard voices directing him what to do. He followed these voices. Most patients got well, although nearly all of them were classified as being medically incurable. If I wanted to learn more of spiritual healing I should get in touch with Maurice Barbanell, the editor of *Two Worlds*, who would be interested in hearing about the healing. He could answer my questions.

I thanked him and turned to leave. My hand was on the door knob when he said something that stopped me dead in my tracks. "Say that again." I turned to face him to make sure I had not misinterpreted his strange announcement. He repeated it. And this simple statement helped to change my entire life.

"You are a healer, too," he emphasised. "A born healer. You can do for others what I have done for you. You are a natural healer."

Jean was excited when I told her. We were dying to try it on our friends. But they all seemed disgustingly healthy. Without wishing any of them harm, I hoped somebody would drop writhing at my feet. Nobody did. It is difficult to be a healer if you have no one to heal. Patiently, I waited.

Maurice Barbanell did not seem very surprised when I telephoned him and told him about how I had been healed, but agreed to have lunch with me. He turned out to be a dapper little man with grey hair, brushed well back, and horn-rimmed spectacles. Over lunch, I told him the whole story. He asked many questions and made copious notes. He thought my having been examined by one of the top consulting physicians immediately before and after the healing gave it a certain authenticity. And he subsequently published a very full and scrupulously accurate report on the front page of *Two Worlds*.

During lunch, I asked him to tell me more about spiritual healing and its implications. He would not agree with Santayana, from whom I quoted "Man is not made to understand life, but to live it". He said we should certainly live it to the full but that we could understand much more than we did.

Maurice Barbanell (or "Barbie", as everybody calls him) is now one of my best friends. He started me on a course of reading that completed the reorientation the healing had commenced. Under his patient and knowledgeable tutelage, I read about Spiritualism, about healing, about psychic phenomena. But something strange was happening.

The books I read were new to me, and so were the authors. Yet I was continually coming upon things I already knew. It was not just facts but a whole spiritual philosophy. The more I read the more I realised I already knew what I was reading. It was like going into a house in a far country you had not previously visited and realising that not only had you been there before but you knew the place intimately.

As sterile and unacceptable as I had found the theology of orthodox religions, so as fruitful and completely true did I find the philosophy of Spiritualism. Later, I shall write on this philosophy. Then, the full impact was still not clear. But I knew in my heart and in my mind that the seemingly miraculous healing I had received had opened a door for me. I had walked, wondering, through that door and found there the garden of truth and understanding I had sought all my life.

CHAPTER SEVEN

THE WHEEL TURNS

IT was cold. It was raining. I had had a full day at the office and I was tired and hungry. Women can be hungry and look happy. Men cannot. At least, I cannot. When I am hungry, I get irritable —what Oliver Wendell Holmes called "Lean, hungry, savage, anti-everything". When I am cold and wet, too, I am just not worth knowing. To cap it all, Jean and the car were not there to meet me and I had to queue for a taxi to take me up to The Droveway House.

As this was to be the chosen time for my first act of healing, it may be relative to record that I was feeling completely unspiritual. I found Jean in the sitting room, propped up in an armchair with her legs up on a stool and in great pain. She had put out her sacroiliac joint—a large joint near the base of her spine.

Our five children are a large, healthy lot. As babies, they were never particularly small or fragile. Picking them up or trying to get a couple out of a bath was often an effort. Jean had done this to herself before. When the sacroiliac is out, there is not much you can do. The last time it had happened, she had to be strapped up and kept immobile for some weeks.

When somebody very dear to you is injured, you tend to get officious. Which is why a mother will chide a child who has hurt himself. "Why aren't you in bed?"I queried. "Why haven't you called a doctor? Why aren't you strapped up and immobilised?"

Jean smiled through her pain. "I was waiting for you to come home. You're a healer. Heal me!"

Well, here it was. My first patient. Overcoming an inclination to have a complete scrub-up and don a white gown, I took off my sodden raincoat and washed my hands. Trying to emulate Fricker, as near as I could, I put my left hand on her stomach and rubbed my right over her lower back. Absolutely nothing happened. I helped her up to bed and repeated the process. Then I made us both supper.

Next morning, she was fine. There was no stiffness, no loss of movement, no pain. I was a healer.

A few months later, in the course of business, I met a lawyer from South Africa. He was a big man—over six feet tall and, I should judge, in his late thirties. He had come to London to deal with some legal matters but also to see the very same specialist whom I had consulted. This man was ill. Two of the vertebrae in his backbone were out of true. For four and a half years he had been in constant pain. As soon as he rose in the morning, he strapped on a massive spinal jacket. He removed it only to go to bed for a heavily drugged sleep. Every movement was agonising. He could walk only a few yards before the pain became unbearable. He could not drive a car, or bend down, or even dress himself. Once he was behind his office desk he could carry on, he told me, but any social life was a great strain. An accomplished athlete, he had given up all sports and lived the chairborne life of a premature invalid.

I showed him the report of my healing in *Two Worlds*. South Africans are very down-to-earth people. If you tried to find the most matter-of-fact of them all, you need go no further than a Johannesburg lawyer. So it was with little hope that I watched him read the account of spiritual healing. But I realised that his being here was no coincidence. He had seen the same specialist as I. The verdict was very definite and without hope. His ailment was incurable. He would have to wear a different kind of spinal jacket, perhaps, and learn to live with it. The doctors in South Africa had said the same thing. He had come to London to see the leading authority as a last hope, and was told that his case was beyond hope. And here was I, offering him a straw to grasp. He said he would like to see Fricker.

Just as, at my moment of hopelessness, a man had offered me a solution I did not know existed, I offered him the same solution. As I telephoned Fricker, I reflected on the ways of providence.

Fortunately, the healer was available. I drove the lawyer myself to the little house in Howard Road. I did not warn the man, and he was surprised indeed at the environment of South Tottenham.

Fricker wasted no time. He immediately and accurately diagnosed the two dislocated vertebrae. Together, we helped the lawyer out of his orthopaedic jacket. Fricker turned to me. "Let's do this one together," he smiled.

As the patient stood there, not understanding, we each placed our left hand on his back. The music from the radiogram welled up. I felt an intense vibration in my right hand. It lasted a few minutes, then faded away. Fricker turned off the music. "For four and a half years you have had two displaced vertebrae. In four and a half minutes you have been healed."

The patient looked dazed. "What can't you do?" he was asked. He could not touch his toes. We told him to try, and he did so without effort or pain. He could not lie down without help. We cleared the two stools out of the way and got him to lie down, roll over a couple of times and get up unaided. He had not been able to do up his shoe-laces for four and a half years. We undid them, and he stooped and did them up.

He stood there, with a look of complete wonderment on his face, trying different movements. His back was free. He could do anything. He was entirely without pain, stiffness or discomfort. He had been healed.

Next day, the lawyer telephoned me at my office. He had walked five miles, looking at London. His wife was exhausted. He was fine.

The following evening, he phoned again. He had walked even farther. His wife had given up and gone to bed to rest. He was going out again on his own to see London by night.

Two days later, he telephoned to thank me again and to say goodbye. No, he was not going back to South Africa. He felt so fit and well, he was going on an extended tour of Europe . . .

Eight months later, he sent me a box of crystallised fruit from Johannesburg with a note telling me had taken up swimming again and felt terrific.

Through all this, I pondered on something Fricker had said as we left. He had shaken hands, looked me in the eye and said very pointedly, "I don't know why you brought him to me. You could have healed him yourself just as easily."

CHAPTER EIGHT

I BECOME A HEALER

"ROLL up! Roll up! Come and visit Tester, the miraculous healer. Incurable diseases treated free of charge. Baffle your doctor. Come and be healed." This was my message. It was clear enough. People in pain, the crippled, and the sick at heart would surely respond. Yet I could not shout it from the housetops. I am, by nature, a retiring man. But even if I had been the world's greatest extrovert, I doubt if I could have "cried my wares". There was a problem to overcome. I was still very uncertain about whether I really could heal.

The 'cons' seemed to outweigh the 'pros'. There were two 'pros'. One was the advice Ted Fricker had given me. He had said I was a born healer. He had told me to heal the sick as I had myself been healed. He had been right when he healed me, in the face of an informed body of medical opinion. Why should he be wrong now?

A smaller 'pro' was the fact that I had healed Jean. But at the moment of healing I had felt nothing. Perhaps she would have got better anyhow. One or two of our friends had let me give them healing for minor ailments, and I had helped Fricker with the South African lawyer. All had become well in a few days. Would their condition have improved naturally?

The biggest 'con' was that I felt no different in myself. When I healed, I did what I had seen Fricker do. I rubbed my right hand over the affected area, and my left hand I kept at rest opposite it. It was as if my left hand was a sort of negative—an earth, in electrical parlance—and the right was the power hand. Amongst the books Barbanell had recommended was one on healing by the greatest spiritual healer of them all, Harry Edwards. He recommended a healer to seek "attunement". I tried. The music helped

—particularly Tschaikovsky's *Nutcracker Suite*. After ten or fifteen minutes, I did drift off a little into a sort of daydream. Was this attunement?

But I felt no difference. I heard no voices, saw no visions, experienced no supernatural phenomena. Was anything happening? Did my friends say they were better just to please me, or were they really well after receiving "treatment"?

You cannot successfully advertise your services—or any products, for that matter—if you have no confidence in them yourself. There were two questions I needed to have answered. First, was I truly a natural, born healer? Secondly, if I was, how did I get patients? My mentor was Barbanell. After all, he was one of the world authorities on Spiritualism and healing and was also a newspaper man. This qualified him to advise me both on my qualifications and how to advertise them. So I asked him. I remember quoting Jefferson's letter to Nathaniel Macon in which he wrote "Advertisements contain the only truth to be relied on in a newspaper".

Barbanell's answer was short. He invited Jean and me to come to his flat in St. John's Wood the following week to attend Hannen Swaffer's home circle. We went.

Hannen Swaffer was, and probably still is, the most colourful personality Fleet Street ever produced. No newspaper man has since surpassed him for sheer showmanship, reportage or journalistic ability. He set out to expose fraudulent mediumship and became, instead, converted to Spiritualism. For many years, a home circle of dedicated men and women sat every week with him to contact those who had passed on to the other world. When he too made the great change we call death, the circle continued. And he remained a member of it.

The circle now met in Barbanell's flat. I knew that the guide who controlled what happened was called Silver Birch. His philosophy was well known to me. The many published books of his teachings I had read again and again. What I did not know was that Barbanell was the medium through whom Silver Birch manifested himself.

Jean and I had never attended a seance before. At the pleasantly furnished flat, we were greeted by Barbanell, his charming wife Sylvia, and a group of six or seven matter-of-fact men and women. Chairs were arranged in an irregular circle round the sitting room. We were allocated seats, with the men and women alternating. Then everybody stood up, placed their hands on a small centre table and raggedly sang a hymn: "Open my Eyes." The table rocked. Each member of the circle welcomed a friend, a relative or a guide from the spirit world. As each name was spoken, the table rocked vigorously.

Then we returned to our chairs. Barbanell sat on the sofa. We all made ourselves comfortable, as he did. He took off his spectacles, drank a little cold water and closed his eyes. Nobody took a blind bit of notice of him. The lights were full on. Everybody chatted happily with his neighbour. For between three or four minutes, we talked of this and that. Then Barbanell groaned, shook his head, sat up and, with his eyes still firmly closed, greeted everyone in the room.

But this was not the Barbanell I knew. His manner was different; his voice was deep, with a strange accent. His vocabulary was unusual. His face had become transformed into that of a lined, incredibly wise and elderly foreigner. It was Barbanell who sat on the sofa. It was Silver Birch who occupied his body and who spoke to Jean and me.

The teachings of Silver Birch have been published in many lands. Some of the books have been put out as paperbacks. I recommend them to you. What he said to us that evening was very personal. He answered many questions that were in our minds, including the all-important one. He told me that my entire life had been a preparation for the task that lay ahead. He told me I had been born to heal.

When he had finished, he asked us if we had any questions. Naturally, I wanted to know how I would get patients. I was told that I was not to worry. The gift of healing would not be wasted. The patients would come.

For everybody in the room, Silver Birch had a message—often intensely personal. To any who asked questions, he supplied precise answers. After over an hour among us, he said his farewells, uttered a short prayer and was gone. Where a strange, dominant and unnaturally wise man had been, we now saw Barbanell slumped on the sofa.

For some minutes we chatted quietly, as you do in the presence

D

of a sleeping child. Then he shuddered, took a deep, deep breath
and opened his eyes. He took another sip of cold water, rubbed
his hand over his face and donned his spectacles. Barbanell was
with us once more.

Throughout, one of the circle had been writing shorthand. I was
told that when she was away they used a tape-recorder. Every
Silver Birch sitting was fully recorded. From these recordings the
books were prepared.

This is not a book about Silver Birch. He is one of the greatest
phenomena of our times. His many books speak for themselves.
But I noticed something at that first meeting. Subsequently, I
confirmed it—because I have met him many times since. Barbanell is a journalist and a writer. He has many books and hundreds
of articles to his credit. His style is clear but characteristic. Like
most experienced and professional writers, he has developed a
personal style. It is as much a part of him as his mode of speech
or the way he walks. And "Style is the man". What I noticed was
that the style of Silver Birch is that of another man. He not only
uses different words, he uses them differently. His vocabulary is
different. The structure of his sentence is different. His whole
literary style is that of a man schooled elsewhere.

Jean and I have now sat with many mediums. But that
first sitting remains a landmark. We went home full of wonder
and remembering all the questions we should have asked but
didn't.

Haywards Heath is not too difficult to reach. We decided to
make it as easy as possible for those wanting healing to find us. I
had my office run off several copies of a form setting out the hours
and times for healing and how to reach The Droveway House.
And Jean had a word with Station Taxis and arranged for them
to collect anybody who came to the station. It was agreed that
they would request no fare from those who did not volunteer it. We
would pay a monthly account.

The time allocated for healing was Monday afternoon, from
two to six o'clock. On my first Monday I put a piano stool in the
drawing room, the *Nutcracker Suite* on the record-player, a bowl
of water and a towel on a trolley next to the door—and I was ready
for the rush of patients.

A business lunch at the Mirabelle with a journalist from *The Financial Times* triggered off the rush.

I deal only with shops and business properties in my profession, but I cover the whole of the United Kingdom. At about this time, my reputation was spreading. There was nothing very dramatic about my work, but sometimes things catch the imagination of the public or the Press. I remember I had purchased the old Y.M.C.A. building in Manchester and was wondering how to develop it profitably. Behind the Victorian sepulchre I had acquired ran the Rochdale canal. And immediately adjoining was a canal basin with lock gates. My idea was to negotiate a building lease over the canal basin, to demolish the Y.M.C.A. and to build a tower block of offices and showrooms over both sites. It was tricky. The deal could only be done if I guaranteed the free flow of canal traffic 365 days a year. The canal banks were "puddled". They were made of compressed wet clay. How to build a large commercial structure with barges running through the basement was problem enough, but it had to take tugs, too.

Among my associates were a clever young architect and a brilliant engineer. Between us, we concocted a structure fourteen storeys high consisting of a series of reinforced concrete frames—like enormously high, flat goal-posts with massive cross-bars. We planned to erect three of these and to sling the building between them. The framework would straddle the canal and the basin, and the first floor would be raised sufficiently to allow barges and tugs to pass below. And it worked.

In architectural and property circles, this created a minor furore. *The Financial Times* ran, and still runs, the most widely-read gossip column in business journalism. It is headed "Men and Matters". I do not know how many men have written this feature, but at that time it was run by a well-known journalist called Robert Heller.

Heller contacted me and said he would like to do a feature—a short "profile", I think he called it. Now, I am all for publicity. But you cannot influence a responsible journalist. He will write what he wishes. All you can do is make sure he sees you in the most congenial atmosphere. I took Robert Heller to the Mirabelle for lunch.

The Mirabelle is in Curzon Street and has the reputation of

being one of the ten best restaurants in Europe. I am not a gourmet, so I cannot judge if this reputation is deserved or not. I do know it is one of the most expensive.

We munched our way through an extensive menu. Heller is an easy man to talk to. I suppose it is part of his professional know-how to be so. A good listener and a memorable meal create the atmosphere for witty talk. I like to think he was amused. Over coffee, he said, "I have enough about your property activities. What do you do outside the office?" I told him I was a spiritual healer.

So it happened that when I was written-up in "Men and Matters" in *The Financial Times*, the last paragraph contained the uncommercial news that I was a healer.

"Let me make the newspaper, and I care not what is preached in the pulpit or what is enacted in Congress." Wendell Phillips was right. From that short paragraph, a snowball started to roll—and to gather in size as it did so.

My local paper is *The Mid-Sussex Times*. It comes out every week. The editor must have seen "Men and Matters", because the following week there was half a column about me. It mentioned healing.

For some years I had been a member of the Cuckfield Urban District Council. Service to my fellow men is an important part of my philosophy. Service in local affairs is something to which we can all contribute. Council meetings were reported by a young bearded Scot called Robin Anderson. I liked him and had often exchanged a few words after a meeting.

He telephoned me after reading the local paper and said he thought *The Argus* might make a feature of me. Could he come up with a photographer on Saturday morning?

The Argus is published every evening in Brighton. It covers a wide area. The following week, nearly a full page was used for Robin Anderson's article. It was headed "A Man in a Million on his way to a Million". There was a photograph of Jean and me on a stone seat, with some of the children in the swimming-pool.

The following weekend a Jaguar pulled up outside the house and a young man from *The People*, the national Sunday newspaper, arrived unannounced to interview us. He stayed quite a while—a habit most of our visitors develop—took many photographs and eventually produced, the next Sunday, a half-page feature about us in *The People*.

Suddenly, I was well known. The *English Digest* carried my story, as did an American magazine. As James Ellis wrote, "Newspapers are the world's mirrors". I was certainly being reflected in them.

Now I had more patients than I could cope with. The publicity in the press brought them from all over England. The large hall at The Droveway House which we used as a waiting room was full to overflowing. There were sick people waiting outside in cars. Cripples were sitting on the stairs. The halt and the lame filled the available chairs. We had to bring more in from the garden.

All this had happened to me. Now it was going to happen to them.

CHAPTER NINE

AN OPENER OF DOORS

NEARLY everyone who comes to me for healing is at the end of a
long line of orthodox medical failure. I am seldom, if ever, asked
to heal a disease that is medically curable. My patients are almost
all "chronic incurables". Tired, worn, emaciated, bent and lame,
they trace a painful pathway towards my quiet room. There they
find hope, understanding and, often, complete healing.

When a man is healed, he wants to learn something of the power
that made him whole again. For such a man, I open a door and
show him the garden that lies beyond. I understand only too well
how he feels.

I, too, have trod the road of pain and known the sheer frustration
of hopelessness. I shall always be grateful to three men: to Tony,
who pointed out a door I did not know existed; to Ted, who opened
it; and to "Barbie", who took me by the hand and led me through
it to find the flowers. There is a French proverb about gratitude
being the heart's memory. My heart remembers.

Now I, too, am sometimes privileged to open the door. As a
spiritual healer, I receive the sick. Those who are ready to be healed
are healed. Many who seek help and guidance receive it. I cannot
measure what I do in numbers. If I open the door to the garden
of spiritual awareness to one, it is enough.

My patients tell me their sorry tales of error and folly. To them,
their histories are unique. To me, recurrent patterns emerge. I console them for their mistakes. "The man who makes no mistakes
does not usually make anything." I quote La Rochefoucauld's:
"He who lives without committing any folly is not so wise as he
thinks." And I offer them all healing. For some, the door opens.

From the wide spectrum of human frailty I experience, I shall
write. In doing so, perhaps I may point out the way to you.

Neither my healing nor my writing is an end. Each is a means. The end is the spread of spiritual truth. "And ye shall know the truth, and the truth shall make you free," said John.

Monday is my healing day at The Droveway House. I keep "open house" from two until six in the afternoon. Jean helps me with the simple preparations. We put an old piano stool in the centre of a Persian rug in the drawing room. Jean wheels in a trolley bearing a bowl of water, soap and a towel. The only other piece of equipment is a tape-recorder on which I play music through a large hi-fi speaker. There are no tapes of sacred music. I play anything I fancy. Sometimes it is Sibelius, sometimes ballet music like the *Nutcracker Suite*; often it is sophisticated jazz.

We have a large hall. This acts as a waiting room when there is a rush on. There is a collecting box for anybody who feels the need to give something. It all goes to the poor. I make no charge. Healing is a gift. I feel it must be free to whoever asks for it.

I have a frugal lunch. A heavy meal inhibits the healing. In any case, I am almost a vegetarian. The word "almost" has been inserted in the interest of complete truthfulness. Sometimes, because of social pressures, I do eat a little fish. After lunch I read, or catch up on my writing, and sip a cup of coffee. By two o'clock there are generally one or two patients waiting. But unless somebody is in pain, I do not start until two.

I walk through the hall. Who is first? A woman gets up and follows me into the drawing room. She is a new patient who has written to me for healing. I asked her to come and see me. I sit her on the stool facing the window and the lovely garden beyond, which is Jean's particular joy. She is told to take off her outer clothes only. I wash my hands and then ask her to tell me her troubles.

Although she has written to me in some detail, I have not kept the letter. I find patients like to tell their own story. Their telling it is a useful prerequisite to healing—a form of mental catharsis, perhaps.

She is sitting in a large quiet room. There are flowers all around her. I keep silent but look sympathetic. The floodgates are about to be opened. I wait. I can see all the symptoms. There is unhappiness, self-pity, a deep sadness approaching melancholia—and

I can sense a feeling of guilt. She takes a handkerchief from her sleeve and starts to talk.

Invariably, patients tell a disjointed history. I help her, ask a few questions, and take her through the difficult part again. She is suffering from severe pains of the shoulder and neck, extending to the head and sometimes around the cheekbone. Her doctor has diagnosed neuritis. Sometimes it feels like toothache, but her dentist assures her that her teeth are all right. The pain is not constant. It comes and goes.

Her husband died last year. She thinks the pain started about six months ago. Their marriage was not happy and she was untrue to him. She has no children, feels alone, abandoned, and has a guilt complex.

When she has finished, I switch on the tape-recorder. I have on it a tape by George Shearing, *Night Mist*. Do you have to be blind to make music like this? I stand behind her as she sits on the stool. My right hand I put on her forehead, my left hand at the back of her neck. I look across to the recorder. On top of the cabinet is a small photograph of Galen, my first healing guide. I close my eyes and let the music help me drift. Almost immediately, I am attuned. I feel a sort of questing power in my fingers. My right hand starts vibrating strongly. This woman is run-down; her resistance is at a low ebb. My hands move of their own accord over her shoulders and neck. There is a great deal of muscular tension.

Gently but firmly, my hands stroke her shoulders and rest on the places where she complained of pain. Gradually, she starts to relax; and I feel the tensions go from her.

All this time my eyes have been closed. Suddenly, they are open. The music comes to the end of a passage and I stop the tape. The healing is finished. The woman seems relaxed and happy. She tells me she is free of pain for the first time for months. Her real problem, I know, is the need of spiritual understanding. I give her a book and ask her to read it and to come and see me the following Monday.

The next in line is a man. He, too, is a new patient. He is about forty. Thin, tall—a little under six feet—he walks very stiffly and is extremely self-conscious. He tells me he has had treatment for over a year for a slipped disc. He has been in plaster, but this has now been removed. He has had traction. The pain and discomfort persist. He has all the classic symptoms—pains in the back and along the line of the sciatic nerve.

I switch on the tape again, nod to Galen, and place my right hand on the small of the man's back. My left hand rests lightly on his stomach. The reaction is immediate and positive. He has a slipped disc all right. It is the one between the fourth and fifth lumbar vertebrae. There is a lot of vibration in the fingers of my right hand. It builds up to a crescendo. I get very hot. Then, suddenly, it is over.

As I turn off the music, I tell him to walk to the bay window and back. He walks swingingly and without stiffness. I tell him to bend down and touch his toes. He does this grudgingly. But suddenly he realises he can now do what I ask. He is all smiles. The pain has gone. He is healed.

I warn him that he will still get sciatic twinges for some weeks. The sciatic nerve takes some time to die down once it is aroused. I ask him to come again in a fortnight so that I may check on his progress. He strides out with wonder in his eyes.

I am washing my hands when in comes the milkman. Rheumatoid arthritis of the hands and wrists brought him to me five weeks ago. He kept dropping the milk bottles. His wrists were badly swollen and he had no grip in his fingers. Now, the wrists are down to normal size and he has his grip back. It is not as strong as it used to be, but good enough to hold a bottle of milk. I finish off the Shearing tape on him. His hands are much stronger. Though there is still muscular weakness to some degree, the arthritis is hardly apparent. I tell him to see me again in two weeks. He goes out a happy man.

I look into the hall. It is empty. I change the tape to Sibelius, push down the pause button and sit down for a few minutes to catch up on my correspondence. People write to me from many countries. Some of the letters run into a number of pages. I reply with sympathy and brevity. If they want healing, I send them a duplicated letter telling how and when to come. If they cannot travel, I try to put them in touch with a healer near their home who can call on them. If they want advice, I give it on the back of a postcard. The postcard, for privacy, goes in an envelope.

I like postcards. There is no preamble; no conventional ending.

The address is printed at the top and my name in the bottom right-hand corner. Between them I can get seven lines of writing. On these seven lines I have to answer a six-page letter. If *I* wrote letters, I could never get ahead of my correspondence. With post-cards it is easy. But you have to learn a pretty compact prose style. If anybody ever bothers to ask who had the greatest influence on my style as a writer, I would unhesitatingly say the Postmaster General. He is the man who dictates the dimensions of post-cards.

I am just finishing my fourth reply when the front-door chimes sound. It must be a new patient. The front door is never locked. Everybody who knows us just charges in. I open the door to a short, portly, fair-haired man of around thirty-five who is blushing like a schoolgirl.

On the stool, he confesses that this is exactly his problem. He cannot stop blushing. He is a keen amateur singer—operatic, too. But whenever he appears in front of an audience, he blushes. Blushing has become a "thing" with him, and it is starting to get him down.

I look at Galen as I turn on the Sibelius tape. It took a long search to get that portrait. There is only one known bust of this "father of modern medicine" and nobody knew where it was. Eventually, I ran down a photograph of it and managed to make a good copy. This Greek physician had made the exciting change we call "death" in 201 A.D. Now he helped me.

This patient is run down and emotionally disturbed but has nothing organically wrong with him. With my hands on his head, I drift off and let the healing forces flow through me. I tell him I think I can help. He has hope now, and he promises to come again next Monday.

I wash my hands, and the next man comes in. He is well over six feet tall and has the width to go with it. I remember him well— eroded disc between 2L and 3L. He came two weeks ago and seemed to respond well. No Sibelius for him. I change the tape for the latest Cy Grant, just to show I am not too square. He tells me diffidently that he is now quite well and that he has experienced no pain since his last visit. He feels so fit that he has only come back because I had insisted that he should.

Galen seems to smile at me as I turn on the mood-music. I run my right hand down the man's back. He seems perfectly fit. I tell him he is healed, but I give caution against possible twinges. I suggest he sees me again for a check-up in a month's time. But I know I will never see him again.

The hall is empty and I go back to my writing. Jean fortifies me with tea. From where I am sitting, I can see the front door. As I start to read the last letter, the door opens and a young woman comes in. I greet her warmly and take her into the drawing room. She is twenty-eight but not over-bright. Her husband has left her. She does not get on with her mother. The neighbours do not like her. She has been a patient in a mental hospital. She thinks she is going to take her own life.

When she came to me originally, six months ago, she said she was on the verge of suicide and was a bundle of misery. She is quite cheerful now and enjoys her weekly visit to me. She only throws the suicide threat at me now and again when she gets frightened that I might tell her she is well and need not come any more.

I give her Cy Grant and generalised healing. She goes away happy. I cannot decide whether I am a charlatan, a substitute father-figure, or an experienced psychologist.

My next patient is a problem. She is suffering from an unusual eye disease and her vision is seriously affected. She has been to see me four times already. There is no apparent change in either her physical or her spiritual condition. She wants to know if she should try some other healer.

I give her the name and address of the secretary of the local healers' association. There are many spiritual healers throughout the country. Most of them are members of The National Federation of Spiritual Healers. The local secretaries keep a list of healers and a note of their availability. Perhaps one of them would be better for her. In any case, I assure her, she must feel free to come and see me whenever she wishes and I will always do whatever I can to help. I give her healing for her eyes. There is no improvement. She leaves me depressed and unhappy. I want to give her hope. But I must not.

Then I am presented with a patient suffering from chronic sinusitis. She tells me that for three years she has been unable to obtain anything other than minor and spasmodic relief. She seems emotionally upset and generally in a poor condition of health. I change tapes and go back to Shearing. She needs soothing.

I put my hands on her head, drift off, and let them investigate. The fingers of my right hand move over the antrum. There, I sense congestion; the tubes are distended and there is some infection. My hand starts to vibrate. The vibration concentrates in my fingers as they rest on her face. A feeling of great heat comes from my hand and penetrates her face. The patient starts to perspire. Then the feeling fades. I am fully awake. I give her a box of tissues and tell her to "have a good blow". I switch off the tape. As I wash my hands, she blows her nose once or twice. A great deal of mucus comes away. She cleans up and tells me she is free of all pain and discomfort and breathing easily and freely for the first time for months. I impress on her the need to see me again in a week. The infection must be cleared up. But we are on the right road, I know.

A wave of exotic perfume heralds a buxom blonde of about thirty-eight with a figure like Venus de Milo. This is enclosed in a pink sweater made for a smaller woman. She smiles happily at me and says she thinks she has cancer of the breast. When she is seated on the stool and persuaded not to strip off, I get Jean in as a chaperon.

A healer is in a very vulnerable position. He has no recognised orthodox medical education or qualifications. The British Medical Council does not acknowledge that he has any position in the world of medicine. The Establishment is unsympathetic to his claims. Whilst those who have been healed are full of praise, those who have no experience of healing are prejudiced against it. A healer must make no claim that he can cure any illness. He must not give healing to a child without making sure the parents are aware the child must not be denied orthodox medical care. He should not treat a pregnant woman. If he is asked to heal any woman, he should be chaperoned.

I use my discretion, as we all must. To new patients I say, "Please understand that I have no recognised orthodox medical qualifications. I offer you healing because I have the gift and I feel it must be shared. I will share it with you freely and accept no fee or other reward of any kind. I promise you nothing. You will please regard this healing session merely as an experiment among friends. If it helps you, I am delighted. If it doesn't, then you have lost nothing."

But if I have to deal with diseases of the breast or the womb, or with any genito-urinary ailments, I get a chaperon.

Jean comes into the drawing room, gives a cheery greeting to Venus and stays near me. I play some music. There is no reaction from the blonde's forehead. She is fit and well. I take a deep breath and lay my hands flat on the spot she indicates. Then I drift away and I do not know if I am healing a buxom blonde, a thin man or a horse. There is no reaction; definitely no cancer. I come round and find Jean watching me like a hawk. My hands investigate the patient's shoulders and neck. She is certainly a well-built girl. There is little wrong. I tell her to see her doctor, get his diagnosis, and come back in a fortnight. It seemed like muscular strain to me. But I did not like to suggest it.

Fifteen minutes on my own and my correspondence is dealt with. I am just sticking on the last stamp when three patients arrive together. They have shared the same taxi from Haywards Heath station. The first is an advanced case of osteo-arthritis of the spine. He has suffered from this painful disease for over fifteen years. There is no hope medically, no treatment that can give him more than marginal relief. His doctors have advised him to "learn to live with it". He does not think he can.

I play some Tschaikovsky and run my hand down his spine. I get a reaction down the full length. This man is in a bad way. I drift off and he gets intense healing down the entire backbone. When it is over, he says his back feels warm and comforting. It still hurts, but the pain has been reduced to a dull ache. He lives in London, so I give him my office address and suggest that he telephones for an appointment there in a week's time. I can help him, but I feel the progress will be slow.

He is followed by a pitiful sight—a young man with a wasted body, emaciated and deformed, hanging on aluminium tubular crutches. He has a form of lymphoma, a terrible wasting disease. Medically, it is invariably terminal. I play Gounod's *Ave Maria*, ask my guide for a lot of power, and go to work on his poor distorted body. It takes a long time. I get reactions from almost every part of him.

I tell him I will do all I can, but I make no prognosis. I give him my telephone number. He may call me whenever he needs strength. He will pass over soon, this one. As he shakes my hand, I can see that he already knows. I hope I can make his passing an easy one. I remember talking to Paul Beard, the principal of The College of Psychic Science, and saying I seemed to be spending much of my life helping people to die. And he replied, "It is one of the most important functions of a healer."

The next patient is positively radiant. Three weeks ago she was depressed, suffered from severe back pains, had a distorted skeleton with one leg shorter than the other, and could not overcome an urgent compulsion to take to her bed and not get up again. Now she is fit and well. She has thrown away the built-up shoe she has worn for years and is completely free of pain. She comes only to thank me. I am delighted at her good health. But I tend to reject thanks. You do not thank a radio-set for giving you a symphony. Thank the man who wrote it; or the orchestra that played it; or God, who inspired it.

It is a quarter to five. The children are home and Jean wheels a trolley laden with sandwiches, cakes and hot buttered scones into the playroom. I join them for tea and spend a pleasant ten minutes with the family I love. I am interrupted by one of my problems.

He is a charming, well-read and highly educated man of about fifty-five. He suffers from chronic insomnia, with all the trimmings. These include colonic spasms, violent headaches, muscular pains and cramp. I know this man is spiritually sick. Yet my healing seems to have given him absolutely no relief.

He comes often to talk, to share my music, and to receive healing. He has been many times. Neither of us can trace a vestige of improvement in his condition. I welcome him, play some Bach, give him healing and discuss philosophy. He goes away happy but firmly convinced he will not sleep a wink tonight. And he is probably right. I tell Galen, "Sometimes I feel helpless."

It is nearly six when my last patient arrives. His wife is seriously ill in hospital with a cerebral haemorrhage. I am to visit her, with her physician's consent. But first I must give healing to the husband. He is suffering from a rare urinary complaint, migraine, and self-pity. I treat all three—the first two with contact healing, the last with some forthright philosophy. Then we leave together for the hospital.

His wife is in a side ward on her own. She lies naked under the sheets. Her body is connected by tubes to some complex clinical equipment. She is being fed, drained and emptied through tubes. Regularly, her body is turned, cleaned and rubbed with alcohol. Otherwise, she receives no treatment. She lies with her eyes wide open. But she does not move and she cannot communicate.

I am aware of a spirit trapped in a cage. Her body has ceased to function properly. Yet it still houses her immortal etheric entity. There are only two possible eventualities. Either the body will be repaired and she will be normal again, or it will be discarded and her spirit released. All I can do is give her the strength to do what has to be done and the serenity to wait until then. I quietly lay my hands on her. Sitting on a hospital chair next to her bed, I drift into a dreamlike state. I try to communicate but I feel nothing. After a while, I say goodbye and leave.

My last patient is in a village about five miles away. She is a happy old lady who sits in an ornate bed in a bright ground-floor room to receive me. She is suffering from a rare muscular disease and has been bedridden for sixteen years. She has some pain and a lot of discomfort. I greet her warmly. We chat for a while. Then I give her healing and she responds well. She tells me the pain is much easier. She is now sleeping better.

It is 7.30 p.m. when I get home. Jean has removed all traces of the clinic, and dinner is ready. I wash, change and sit down to a simple evening meal. Another healing day is over.

CHAPTER TEN

SPIRITUAL HEALING WORKS

SPIRITUAL healing works. It works with functional diseases as well as psychosomatic ones. In fact, those ailments that are purely mechanical heal easiest.

One of my patients was called Grazionella Smith. She was a large good-looking Italian girl married to an Englishman. She arrived at The Droveway House after lunch one Sunday. I do not normally heal on Sundays. This is not because I have any sabbatical inhibitions but because it is the day I devote to my family. But this woman was in trouble, in pain, and threatening to end it all by suicide. She was desperate—at the end of her tether and tormented.

I sat her on the stool and waited. She dried her eyes and started to tell her history. Several times I had to take her back over a passage I could not follow. Then I had the whole tale.

She was a school teacher, happily married, with two small sons. When the youngest was born, some four and a half years ago, she had dislocated her right hip in childbirth. It had been manipulated back under an anaesthetic but, because it kept coming out again, the treatment had been repeated a number of times. For over four years she had endured pain and discomfort. The orthodox medical treatment seemed powerless to remedy the trouble for more than a day or two. She could not stand the agony any longer. Would I please, please heal her . . .

She was a large girl, with the wide swinging hips of the southern Italian. I put my hand on her hip and sought attunement. She was too well covered for me to feel the hip-bone, but there was a very strong reaction and she said the pain had lessened. I made her sit quietly for a few minutes. Then, at my suggestion, she walked—timidly, at first—up and down the long room. As her face lit up with the realisation that she was healed at last, her stride lengthened. With her head up, her eyes sparkling, and her hips swinging in the manner only southern Italian women and Bantu water-carrying girls know, she looked terrific.

She came again some time later to show me how wonderfully fit she was; to thank me; and to give me from her bracelet a gold red-pepper charm, which I still have.

Are there any limitations to spiritual healing? I know of only one. I cannot heal what is not there. If a man has been in an accident and has his foot amputated, no healer could make another grow. Patients who have had surgery come for healing when they discover they are still not well. No healer can heal a lung that has been removed, a hip that has been pinned, an organ that has been cut away.

Subject to that obvious restriction, healing is available to everybody who asks for it and for any disease, illness, ailment and deformity.

How does healing work?

I am a spiritual healer. This means that I have been given a gift—like the gift of music or painting or poetry. And like these, it comes from outside me. I am merely a receiving set—a channel through which the great life force can find a path.

I heal best when I do not try to heal. I leave it to my guides. These are spirit people who have made the great change we call death but who wish, for various reasons, to spend some time helping those who are still in this world. The band of healers is headed by Galen, who whilst here was a great Greek physician. And there are others who help me, less famous but experts in specialised fields.

When I heal, I seek attunement with them. It is not an experience that is easy to describe. I do not go into a deep trance. Nor do I employ any ritual, make magic passes, or use any traditional formula. The state I get into is almost like a daydream. The room I am in, the music I sometimes play, and the environment remain known to me. I do not lose consciousness. But I seem to drift away and become aware of something else.

In my writing, I try to be precise. The word "something" strikes me—as it probably does you—as being weak, woolly and vague. Yet if I use another word, I am being inexact. If I say I am aware of a "presence", this is untrue. I am not aware of a person or an entity. "Atmosphere" or "etheric personality" or "power aura" are just words. Perhaps I can be most true if I say that there is a moment when I realise the patient and I are no longer alone.

The patient has already told me, in some detail, the history of his ailment. I listen, ask questions and make sure I have a clear picture of the disease. This is important. The healing life force is around us all the time. It has to be directed. It is essential to know exactly where it is needed. Often, of course, the patient himself does not know. He will complain of sciatica in the leg. But this may be caused by pressure in the lumbar area, and it is to there that the healing force must be directed.

Getting the full picture is important for another reason. Galen is listening. It is he who controls the team of helpers, chooses the spirit doctor who specialises in this type of ailment, and directs the healing force. I am just the instrument through which they work. That is why I must not try too hard.

My responsibility is simple. I have to keep the channel of healing open and immaculate. I practise a high standard of personal bodily and mental hygiene. I eat frugally; I do not smoke; I do not drink. A healing day finds me relaxed, free of business or domestic matters, in radiant health, with my body uninhibited by rich food, tobacco, drugs or alcohol. In this condition, the guides find me a suitable medium through which the healing force can flow to those who need it and are ready to receive it.

It is my sincerest wish that I may thus continue.

She was just short of forty—dark, slim and about five feet seven. Nobody could call her beautiful, but she was comely, clean and neatly dressed. She sat on the stool and whispered. I asked her to speak up. There was a lot of throat-clearing. I said nothing. I have a quality of stillness that produces better results than words. Eventually, she stopped fidgeting, looked me squarely in the face and told me her sorry history.

For nearly two years she had been in discomfort and some pain from a duodenal ulcer. The usual drug and dietary therapy had produced no improvement. She had taken tranquillisers in massive doses, had lived on a regimen of milk, boiled fish and poached eggs and, in spite of all this, was now facing the prospects of surgery.

She was terrified. The thought of going into hospital for an operation frightened her so much that the pain had worsened and she was sleeping badly. She wanted to know if I could heal her and how she could avoid the dreaded operation.

It is not unusual for a healer to be asked to give advice on medical treatment, the use of drugs, the wearing of surgical appliances, or the inevitability of an operation. I never give medical advice. It is not my function. I do not have the requisite qualifications. But I do explain the healing process and the philosophy that surrounds it. And somewhere along the line, the questions all answer themselves.

My patient was now a little more relaxed. I knew the ulcer was the result of stress. Now I sought the cause.

Soon I had the full picture. Her husband had died three years earlier. His death at middle age was sudden and unexpected. She was left with three teenage children and responsibilities she found difficult to bear. The shock of premature widowhood, added to the worry of bringing up and providing for her family unaided, proved too much. She developed what I recognised as classic stress symptoms. The ulcer was the result.

The music of Mozart seemed to relax her. I put my right hand on the top of her stomach and my left hand on her back. My conscious mind shut itself off as the power flowed through me. At these moments, I lose an appreciation of time. I had no idea if I had been "out" for a few seconds or for many minutes. Later, I realised it must have been quite a while because there was a lot of tape on the take-up spool.

She sat quite still, with her eyes closed. The nervousness had left her. She seemed completely relaxed. When she opened her eyes, she was almost serene. For a while, she said nothing. Then she smiled. It was the first smile I had seen. The lines of tension were gone.

I asked her about the pain in her chest. There was none. There was no discomfort, either. She felt fine.

Her programme was to visit the hospital in ten days' time for a barium meal and an X-ray. A week later, she was to see the surgeon for a pre-operative examination.

I arranged for her to come and see me again the next week. As she left, she asked me if I thought the operation would now be necessary. I said I did not know. She asked if she should keep to her bland diet. I said it was up to her.

The following Monday, she was a changed woman. She came in smiling and full of good news. She had been completely free of pain and discomfort for a week. She was sleeping right through the night and eating "like a horse". For the first time in years, she had eaten fish and chips.

We kept up the healing until the surgeon's examination. He told her the X-rays showed no ulcer but only a slight evidence of scar tissue. Hers was not a case for surgery—or for any other treatment, for that matter. He advised her to forget she had ever been ill, to lead a normal life, and to eat whatever she fancied.

When she came to thank me, we talked for a while on spiritual philosophy. She asked for some guidance and I recommended one or two books. The physical change in her was as marked as the philosophical reorientation. She would not develop another ulcer. She was healed.

Sometimes the aftermath of healing is not so clear cut. His name was Lauceston—Roderick Lauceston. He was an engineer employed by a large manufacturing firm in Wales. He used a business visit to London as an opportunity to come and see me at my office. He had a badly prolapsed lumbar disc with all the trimmings— backache, sciatica, distorted hip, lack of mobility. He asked for healing only after assuring me that he had no faith.

His history was conventional. For three years he had suffered the symptoms I knew so well. He had had traction. He now got along on pain-killers and a canvas-and-steel orthopaedic jacket. He had to drive a lot in his job. Some days he reached home exhausted.

The healing was conventional, too. I put my right hand on the lumbar area, my left hand on his abdomen and felt myself fading away as the healing started. But this was no relaxed effort. I was aware of intense activity as my hand worked its way up his backbone to the neck and back again, stopping at each disc and vertebrae. Then it was over.

He was supple and free of stiffness. There was no pain, but only a mild residual sciatica.

As his next business visit to London had not yet been arranged, he did not know when he would be able to see me again. In fact, it was a month later when he called for his final healing. There was nothing much to do. He had full mobility, no distortion, no pain and only minor sciatic aches in his leg. These were spasmodic, and were fading both in intensity and regularity. He was healed.

Five weeks later, I was surprised to see his name on my appointment list. From the way he strode into my room, I knew there was nothing wrong with him. He had come not for healing but for information.

He felt so fit and well that he was determined to find out what had been done to him. Since his last visit, he had arranged privately to see the top orthopaedic specialist in Wales. He had had a new set of X-rays taken. He was subjected to a thorough examination. The specialist had said he did not know why he had been consulted. The X-rays and the examination had yielded the same diagnosis. Roderick Lauceston did not have a prolapsed disc, or anything else wrong orthopaedically—nor, as far as the specialist could tell, had there ever been anything wrong. His spine was perfect. And Lauceston wanted to know what had happened.

The more I heal the less important I seem. I am an instrument. I told Lauceston this and something of the process of healing. For him, too, I recommended a course of reading. This man was an engineer. He appreciated something of the construction of the human skeleton. He knew the stresses and strains a prolapsed disc could set up. His mind could easily grasp the mechanics of the cure, but it could not comprehend either the power or the direction of the force that made it possible. He went away determined to read all that I had recommended in an effort to find out.

Normally, when I have a complete cure followed by this type of reorientation I feel the case is closed. Yet two months later, his name was back on my appointment list. He sat at my desk, completely relaxed and quiet. His back was fine. No, he had had no repetition of the spinal trouble. He was healed—completely healed. He accepted it. What he found difficulty in accepting was the great change in attitude he now experienced.

Where he had been aggressive, he was now passive. Where he had been turbulent, he was now serene. Where he had been resentful, he was now philosophical. He was a changed man. Why? What had happened to him? He wanted to know.

When healing is so successful, it is because there has been a spiritual reorientation. The healing is not an end; it is a means. Lauceston had been spun round. His soul had been exposed; his psyche had been reorientated. He could never be the same again— any more than I could.

With him, too, it went deeper. From what he told me, I realised he was a sensitive. He had a feeling of direction, of guidance. Often, he recognised a place or a pattern of events although he had no pre-knowledge. This man was psychic. He needed help and encouragement. His gift needed to be developed and controlled. I told him not to worry. What he now had was a gift, a wonderful gift. I sent him to those who would help him apply it.

CHAPTER ELEVEN

MAKE YOURSELF WELL

TUESDAY is my healing day in London. I do no professional work on that day. When I arrive at the office I do go through the morning's post. I may dictate one or two letters if they are urgent. Then I have a cup of coffee, wash my hands, and I am ready for the first patient.

My office is a pleasant, bright room on the ground floor of a building near Portman Square. The large windows face west and the afternoon sun floods in, to be reflected back by a wall mirror over a polished chiffonier. The walls are pale grey, the carpet is a deeper grey and the full-length drapes are lime yellow. The Adam fireplace is marble and the furniture Regency. The colour scheme is relieved only by the dark crimson of two comfortable armchairs.

Most of the people who come to see me in London are business men and women. So I give each a definite appointment and try to stick to it. I see patients at half-hour intervals throughout the day, although I have an hour's break at lunch time. If anybody is in pain or is distressed, however, I manage to fit them in. This means I sometimes get down to fifteen-minute sessions. But I manage. And even in this short time, most patients show a definite improvement.

There is, of course, no such thing as a successful or unsuccessful healer. There are only successful or unsuccessful patients.

For some time, I did try to analyse the results of my healing. But there were so many factors of which I could not be fully aware, and so many avenues I could not explore, that I realised the futility of the investigation.

One fact did emerge, however, with blinding clarity. Most of the patients who come to me for healing and who receive a complete and permanent cure have experienced a long history of pain and suffering. Each is "at the end of his tether".

Healing is available to anybody who asks for it. But the patient's ability to receive it varies greatly from person to person— although I doubt if anybody goes away from a healing session without benefit of some kind. You do not have to be racked with pain or on the verge of a nervous breakdown to get help. But there is no doubt that those who have suffered most, and who feel they can tolerate little more physical or emotional stress, are the ones most likely to experience a complete cure.

It does seem that when the human cup has been emptied it is then more easily able to be completely refilled. As I have said, healing is not an end. It is a means.

A man has been in pain for years. He has suffered mental anguish and discomfort. He has become discouraged, disabled and virtually unemployable. He has been told that his ailment is incurable and he must "learn to live with it".

At the end of his tether, on the verge of moral and physical collapse, he goes, as a last desperate measure, to a healer. The healer lays his hands on the racked and painful body. The man is made upright, free of pain. Suddenly and completely, he is healed.

At that moment, his soul is touched. He is spiritually reorientated. For the first time, he is facing the right way—pointing in the right direction along the right road.

At that instant, a man knows his moment of supreme revelation. His life is forever changed and given meaning. Healing is the means of bringing this about.

Those who are in pain, diseased, weary and worn; those who are disillusioned, lacking in the will to go on; those who cannot "learn to live with it"; those who feel they are at the end of the wrong road—take heart. When you have reached rock bottom, there is only one way to go—and that is upwards.

If your cup is quite empty, then lift up your eyes. For it is now in the ideal condition to be completely and permanently filled.

The oldest and most widely used method of treatment of illness is self-medication. There are hundreds of drugs, medicines, remedies and elixirs on sale without prescription. Many are extensively advertised, and their manufacturers have made fortunes. Yet a man who will regularly fill his body with pills and powders seems incapable of any form of spiritual self-prescription.

Nearly all the patients who come to me seem to have made no effort whatsoever to help themselves except by means of orthodox drug therapy. They are all poor in body, in mind and in spirit. Some may enjoy the outward trappings of wealth, but they are nearly all spiritually impoverished.

I try not to preach to my patients. My job, as I see it, is to heal those who are ready to be healed. If, when they have been made well, they want to know more of the forces that healed them, then I am equipped to show them the road they need to travel.

But more and more often I find myself accepting new patients who could heal themselves if only they would alter their attitudes. William James said: "The greatest discovery of my generation is that human beings can alter their lives by altering their attitudes of mind."

I doubt if words will convince you. You will have to want to try it, and then you will find you have convinced yourself. I guarantee that it works. Think positive, optimistic thoughts and you will become well and happy. Think negative, pessimistic thoughts and you will become unhappy and ill.

James was right. It is a discovery, however, not of his generation but of all time.

Take Sam Sloane, for instance. He was middle-aged but looked older. His hair was grey, his posture stooped; his eyes were defeated, and his manner was apologetic. In one body he presented a wide variety of symptoms. He had an ulcer, backache, migraine and a heart condition. He had recurrent pains everywhere. On top of this, he could not sleep. As the long list of ailments was unfolded in detail, it seemed amazing to me that he had somehow managed to avoid bubonic plague and housemaid's-knee.

The man was ill. His pain and insomnia were very real. Yet his ailments were all psychosomatic—the results of stress.

I encouraged him to talk. The sorry tale emerged of failure in business, followed by eight years in a job he loathed but had not the courage to quit. Poor man. He was trying to give his family security. Instead, they suffered the insecurity of a sick provider, an unhappy environment and the constant aura of pessimism.

I gave him healing, of course. But what he needed was education. I hoped he would come back and that he would let me help him. I get many patients like him. They seem to have lost the ability to enjoy life. To them, it is a miserable task instead of a grand adventure. Their constant concern with money, material wealth and social status blinds them to the greater needs of love, laughter and the pursuit of happiness. It was Israel Zangwill who wrote, "Let us start a new religion with one commandment, 'Enjoy Thyself'."

It is his constant search for security that undermines the health of Western man. He becomes ill, endures aches and pains, and substantially shortens his life's span by working at a job he dislikes simply because of the pension at the end of it. Or he succumbs physically and spiritually to the fanatical rat-race of greater and greater material gain. He makes his family unhappy—his children discontented and his wife prematurely old in an atmosphere of tension and the eternal worry of tomorrow.

Yet the remedy lies at his hand. Whatever his philosophy, whatever orthodoxy in his childhood moulded his thought-process and his prejudices, he has ready access to a design for living that provides the complete remedy: Trust God and live one day at a time.

It is perhaps the measure of the failure of Western religions that given this universal remedy they have been unable to persuade their adherents to apply it.

The diseases I am asked to heal cover a wide spectrum, from headaches to cancer, from major orthopaedic dislocations to congenital deformities. My patients come from all walks of life. Some are rich, many are poor. Some are highly educated, others have only a rudimentary learning. Some are spiritually aware, many are in the dark. Yet a pattern always emerges.

People who are ill appear to fall into two distinct categories. Regardless of their pains, their deformities and the sheer inconvenience of their ailments, either they have retained some capacity to enjoy life or they have lost it. Those who can still enjoy life generally get well. Those who cannot seldom do. That is, unless I can reorientate them.

As a healer, I have no pre-knowledge of who will get better and who will not. But I do try to give all patients the fullest opportunity to respond to the healing they receive through me. One way to achieve this is to introduce them to a discovery I have made. It may not be original. Probably, others have made it at different times and in other circumstances. But to me it has all the freshness of a new idea.

Your body's control mechanism responds to your attitude. When you are angry or afraid, your whole metabolism changes. You suffer from high blood pressure, increased pulse rate, high blood clotting factor, muscular tension, and even vocal or muscular paralysis. Nothing physical need have happened to you. It is your attitude that triggers off these reactions. And it is your change of attitude that allows everything to return to normal. It is your attitude, and your attitude alone, that inhibits your body's control mechanism.

Here is my discovery: you can control your body by an artificially induced attitude even if you know it to be false. As anger and fear produce the reactions that induce strain and illness, so do happiness and optimism create health and tranquillity. If, therefore, instead of being fearful and miserable you show all the symptoms of confidence and happiness, your body will adjust itself to these attitudes—even if, in your mind, you know them to be false and purposely simulated.

Try it. Now—at this instant—stop whatever you are doing. Pause. Decide now that for the next hour, and for that hour only, you will exhibit all the symptoms of a supremely happy person. Smile, laugh, sing. Tell everybody that you feel fine, that it is a lovely day, that the world is a wonderful place, and that you have never felt happier. Do this for one hour.

Never mind if you do not believe it. Adopt this attitude. Your body's control mechanism will react. It will say to itself: "He is happy and well. He does not need more blood pressure, more oxygen, more adrenalin, more acid, more defences. He is well and happy. I will stop over-manufacturing the chemicals of bodily defence and restore a harmonious balance to the body." And so it will.

In less than an hour, you will feel fine. In a surprisingly short time, this therapy will convert the imbalance that is making you ill into a harmony that keeps you well.

I repeat, your attitudes control your bodily condition. You can change the condition from misery and disease to happiness and health by altering your attitude—even if, initially, you know it to be simulated.

That is my discovery. It has changed the lives of many. It will work for you. Try it now.

CHAPTER TWELVE

WHAT ABOUT THE CHILDREN?

MOST parents would like their children to carry on where they leave off. To this end, they scrape and save to give them a better education, worry and strive to get them through a university or technical apprenticeship, scheme and wrangle to get them the "right" introductions, nudge and push them into a "suitable" marriage, and become frugal and mean in an effort to leave them a "nest egg" when they die.

I get a lot of patients who are parents of this kind. Arthritis, early hardening of the arteries, insomnia, ulcers, migraine and a wide variety of backaches are a few of their many prevalent diseases. Several times a week I am asked to heal a patient with one of these disease who, superficially, may not seem to be experiencing stress conditions.

Take Mrs. Rother. She is thirty-eight, well dressed and attractive. She admits to having a fine man for a husband, a comfortable home, no serious money problems, and three normal, healthy children. Yet she has worked herself into a condition of serious illness.

Why? Well, the children will need to go to university. Her eldest boy thinks of nothing but girls. Her daughter is mad about clothes. And this she worries about. Maybe the children will get university scholarships. And if they don't, is it such a terrible thing? I can list over a hundred successful men who had only a rudimentary academic education. Her son runs after girls. It seems natural enough to me. If he preferred boys, maybe her concern would be justified. And the girl loves clothes. So did Coco Chanel—and she did just fine.

You cannot live your children's lives for them. They cannot carry on where you leave off. They have to make their own mistakes. They need them as an important step in their learning process. They need the lessons their growing-pains bring. Their joys, frustrations, triumphs, tragedies, successes and failures all contribute to their eventual maturity.

Mrs. Smitherson, another patient, was suffering from acute and painful fibrositis of the shoulder. This condition was so bad that she had become irritable, lost her temper easily, and took to her bed whenever "things became too much". Her pain was real enough. But the cause was psychosomatic. She was literally worried sick because of the financial problems of sending her two sons to the public school their father had been to.

I asked her what choice her sons would make if it was up to them. Would they want an unhappy home continually conditioned by financial crises, sick parents, an atmosphere of stress, and a public school education? Or would they prefer a happy, carefree home, healthy laughing parents, no financial burden, and a local grammar school education?

The choice is obvious. But what *should* we do for our children? What is our responsibility?

Parents should provide bodily comforts. The essentials are a good home, warmth, fresh food, cleanliness, suitable clothing. Home should be a place where every member of the family has a sense of belonging—a haven, a base.

But this is not enough. Children must be loved. The biggest factor in the creation of problem children is the absence of love. It has been clinically proved that love is the greatest single stimulus to a child's development. Your child needs to be kissed, fondled and touched every day. The sense of touch is most important. Tactile relationships have not yet been fully investigated, but we do know that if two people touch one another several times a day a most rewarding human relationship is promoted.

Try it, if you doubt me. Take a person close to you. Use every opportunity to touch him gently. Within a singularly short time, you will find a remarkable improvement in your relationship.

Show your loving in other ways. Be understanding, sympathetic and genuinely interested in your children's problems.

You also need to educate your children. I know they go to school. But there they cannot learn everything. Some things they can learn only from you. Teach them, by your example, to be kind and considerate; to look for the good in people, not the bad. Show them how envy, anger, hate and jealousy hurt those who display these feelings as much as those against whom they are directed. Tell them how they were born, why they are here, what happens when they die. Give them the strength of a true spiritual philosophy. Make them aware of the help and guidance they can receive from their guides. Let them understand something of spiritual healing, the naturalness of health, the value of clean living and right thinking.

Teach your children to recognise right and wrong; to do unto others as they would have others do unto them; to accept their trusteeship for the animal world; to value life, love and laughter above material possessions.

When you have done this, let them live their own lives. Do not interfere. But when they seek help, guidance, comfort—then be readily available.

This is the extent of your responsibility as a parent. You cannot do more. Trying to do so inhibits your child's development. Follow this pattern, and yours will be a house founded on a rock.

CHAPTER THIRTEEN

THE DUMB SING

MY patient made strange moaning noises at me. Her eyes pleaded for understanding but her mouth conveyed only animal sounds. She was about forty, well dressed, and apparently in a good state of preservation. She was accompanied by another woman, who acted as an interpreter. From her, I got the full story.

The patient was childless. Her sole interest in life had been her husband. For him she had kept the small apartment spotless, cooked splendid meals and been an ideal housewife. She had laundered his shirts with the precise care of a craftsman, consulted cookery books so as to make her cuisine interesting and appetising, and constantly thought out new ways in which to make him happy. She had few friends, no hobbies and no outside interests. Her husband had been her life.

Then he died. Suddenly, without warning, he was not there any more. She suffered paroxysms of grief, followed by a mental breakdown. When she eventually recovered, she was dumb. She carried a pad and a pencil and wrote down her needs, or indicated them by gestures. But her doctors could find nothing wrong with her vocal cords. It was as though she had made up her mind that if she could not speak to her husband she would speak to no one. The diagnosis was "hysterical dumbness".

This was the woman who now stood before me . . .

I have had many patients with varying symptoms and different ailments stemming from the same psychosomatic origin—grief. These have included partial paralysis, colitis, insomnia, migraine, backache, sinusitis, fibrositis and psoraisis. The ailments may be different, but the pattern that produced them is generally easily recognisable.

The passing of someone near is followed by intense grief and

The Droveway House, Haywards Heath, Sussex

M. H. Tester at home. The arms of Tester can be seen over the mantelpiece.

then a period of formal mourning. Patients find themselves unable to regain their former vigour. They find they cannot sleep, and they complain of lack of appetite. They start to exhibit the stress symptoms that every healer knows only too well.

I always listen with compassion and understanding as the strangely familiar story is unfolded. It reveals the deeply felt sensations of guilt and self-pity. The guilt is there because people remember all the things they might have done. They recall the times they could have behaved better, been kinder, shown more understanding. Now it is too late. The guilt and remorse are coloured by self-pity, by grief, by denial and the modern equivalent of sackcloth and ashes.

These people do not need healing. They need education.

When somebody close to you dies, he goes to the next world. His life here, and the education it provided, is finished. He enters upon a greater life and a higher education.

There are children who are afraid to leave school because it provides a safe, secure and familiar environment. The world out-side—the world of financial and adult responsibility—is unknown. It is feared. It seems fraught with danger. Yet the child must leave school. His education there is over. He has to pass on to university, to technical training and, inevitably, to the best school of all—the college of personal practical experience.

You, too, will have to leave school one day. This world may be a poor one, but it is the one you understand; the one you have learned to accept. Here, you feel secure. It is the next world that holds the strangeness of the unknown.

The unknown is invariably a little fearful. You may have heard about hell, eternal damnation, punishment, the fiery furnace and the devils that will torment you forever because you have not be-haved like a saint. You are afraid of death.

If this picture were a true one, we would all be afraid—and justifiably so. But the picture is false. The next world is a kindly place full of life, light, happiness and understanding. No person who has died can look back and want to return to this world, any more than a university student would want to return to his primary school.

In the next world, you review the life you led in this one. You consider the mistakes you made, the things you left undone, the

F

good things and the bad. You summarise the benefits you have experienced spiritually by being aware of these things. It is you who sit in judgment. You judge yourself. The lesson is learned. There is no punishment; no childish chastisement. In the spirit world, you have the responsibilities and the knowledge of an evolved adult. You are surrounded by friends who love you. You are free of all pain and suffering, enjoying radiant health, mental tranquillity, and a supreme sense of well being. You look upon the world you have left: and what do you see?

Those who were close to you are crying and wailing. They are dressed in black. They are beating their breasts. They are full of remorse and self-pity. They are denying themselves simple pleasures as a form of penitence.

You wonder at their ignorance, and you pity them. You are filled with compassion for their lack of awareness, for their barbaric superstitions, for their stupidity. But you console yourself with the knowledge that one day you will be reunited. Then you will be able to explain it all to their poor tortured minds . . .

I sat the poor dumb woman on the stool and let the strains of Rossini's *La Cambiale di Matrimonio* overture sweep over her. My hands rested first on her head, then on her shoulders and then on her throat. There was intense vibration as the music swelled. Then it was over. Her shoulders were shaking and she was racked with sobs. The tears poured down her face as she gave way to a paroxysm of emotion.

When she had quietened down and dried her eyes, I put my hand under her chin and raised it up so that her eyes could meet mine. "Sing," I said. "Don't try to talk. Sing. Just one clear note." And she did.

Mrs. de Kock had an abdominal growth. It had been diagnosed whilst she was on a visit to London from South Africa. The doctors were uncertain as to whether it was malignant or benign. She was returning by sea; and when she got home, she would have a biopsy. The subsequent treatment, or an operation for the removal of the growth, would depend on this investigation. She had heard of me. Could she come for healing?

This is what her letter said. But it was incorrectly addressed, and it arrived at The Droveway House twenty-four hours before she was due to sail. By this time, she would have left her London apartment and would be in an hotel in Southampton.

I wrote her a letter and sent it express to the Union Castle Line ship at Southampton. Then I gave her absent healing.

Three weeks later, I had an air mail letter from Cape Town. It told me that Mrs. de Kock had been in some pain when she boarded the ship. Over the next three or four days, however, the pain and the discomfort had gradually subsided. On the fifth day, she had woken up to find that not only was she free of pain but she could not feel the growth. It seemed that it was no longer there. For the rest of the voyage, she had enjoyed excellent health and had joined in deck games and sports on board. On her arrival at Cape Town, she had seen her doctor and a specialist. The X-ray and their examination had disclosed that there was no growth. It had dispersed. She was healed.

Absent healing works. It is the name given to a method of spiritual healing now being widely practised. The healer does not meet the patient. The healing is directed from a distance.

When contact healing takes place, the healer is aware of the patient, of his symptoms, of his distress. He places his hands in contact with the patient's body. His guides direct the healing forces through him. The patient is healed . . . But it is nothing like as simple as that. More than half the sufferers who come to me seem to experience no benefit when they are with me. The next time I see them, they are much improved or even completely healed. Invariably, the pattern is the same. They leave me, feeling uplifted but still with the symptoms they brought with them. Two or three days later, they wake up and realise that the pain has gone; the distressing symptoms have cleared up; they are well.

From this oft-repeated pattern, I can only assume that what happens is this. At the moment of contact, the healing guides are made aware of the ailment. They feel some opposition, some psychic block on the part of the sufferer. They decide they can work best when the patient is asleep and unresisting. A few nights later, when he is in a sleep of a depth and quality they need, the guides carry out the healing process. The patient is made well and wakes up cured.

I have asked them and they have confirmed that this is what

happens. It therefore follows that, if the healing can and does take place when the healer is absent, the direction can also be done from afar. In the spirit world there is a different concept of time and place. Dispersing a growth in the stomach of a woman on board a ship in mid-Atlantic is no more difficult than healing the man next door.

Does this sound strange in a world where an athletic event on the other side of this planet can be photographed and the pictures converted into electrical energy which is then beamed to an artificial satellite encircling the globe, bounced back to a receiving station here, reformed and broadcast on a television wavelength, received and converted into sound and vision by a box in your own home, thus to enable you to witness the event as it is happening?

For absent healing to work, there must be some connection between patient and healer and a definite direction from healer to guide. The first is generally achieved by a letter. I ask sufferers to keep their letters short. But many cannot do this. Some are lonely and need a sympathetic ear. The letter is often their only way of "getting it out of the system". I read all letters addressed to me, however long. What I am looking for is a detailed description of the symptoms or a precise diagnosis. Then I reply, shortly, on one side of a postcard. I thank them for getting in touch with me, assure them they will be given absent healing and ask them to report their progress in a week, a fortnight or a month.

This reporting back is essential. I must be told how the healing is progressing; whether the emphasis need be shifted; when the healing can be terminated. It may be, for instance, that a man suffering from a slipped disc reports that his back is healed, that he is now free of pain there and that full flexibility of the spine has been restored. Yet he may have pain from residual sciatica. The healing will therefore be redirected to the sciatic nerve in his leg.

Surprisingly often, I get letters from ex-patients asking for healing for a friend or relative. A note may start, "Last year you successfully healed me of a lung disease . . ." But I would have had no previous letter from this patient telling me that she had been healed. Perhaps patients think I know. I don't. I have to be told.

The regularity with which I need a report from a patient depends on the ailment and the urgency of a cure. If a man is seriously ill I need to keep in almost hourly touch, and the telephone is used. I need not talk to the man himself, but I do need reports from somebody close to him.

Absent healing must not be confused with prayer. It is not prayer. It is a thought process.

In absent healing, I seek attunement with my guides in the same way that I would if the patient were present. In my thoughts, I visualise the ailment and "picturise" the cure. I give the guides the sufferer's name and address. There is no doubt that an affinity can exist between the mind of a person here and that of a spirit entity. The Archbishop's Commission, formed by Dr. Lang, admitted this. It is this affinity, and his ability to induce it, that is the gift a spiritual healer enjoys.

When you pray, you talk to God. Nearly all prayers are selfish. You achieve nothing, other than the comfort of familiarity, when you recite set prayers There is only one theme worthy of prayer. It is "Thy will be done". Do not tell God what to do. He knows. Just thank Him for your blessings, try and understand His will so that you may follow it, and report for duty. To do this, you need no special building, no special words, no priest, no rituals, no set times. Report in whenever you have a moment to spare. Report in at the end of each day. Keep in touch.

It is perhaps one of the primary causes of the failure of orthodox religion that priests are chosen for their administrative or theological abilities rather than for their psychic powers. When prayers for the sick are given in an orthodox place of worship where the priest is not a natural healer, they are useless. If faith and prayer alone were able to produce healing, we should see it manifested at Lourdes.

There, the whole purpose is to heal the sick. The pomp, the power, the faith and the majesty of the Catholic Church is there focused on the healing act. Cardinals, bishops, dozens of priests, hundreds of nuns and thousands of worshippers are gathered together in almost continual prayer to heal the sick. The enormous power of the Catholic Church, with the blind faith it has learned to generate, is concentrated on this place of pilgrimage. For a hundred years, millions of sufferers have visited Lourdes. If prayer

were enough, surely there would be more healing than the few
dozen cures on record.

I am a member of the local ciné society. Photography is one of
my hobbies. A lady member produced an excellent film of Lourdes.
She had gone as a voluntary helper with a coach-load of handicapped children. The film—in colour, and with a commentary,
sound effects and sacred background music—was very good. You
could feel the audience's sympathy for those deformed children
in wheelchairs and on crutches. You could not but admire their
cheerfulness in adversity as they struggled around Lourdes, ad-
mired the statues and spent their pocket-money on souvenirs. The
photography of the procession was particularly fine—especially
the scene at night, when the thousands of candles borne by the
pilgrims were like myriads of fireflies in the darkness as the moving
chanting washed over them.

When the film was over and the lights were up again, I con-
gratulated the photographer. "Were any of the children healed?"
I asked.

She looked at me as though I had uttered a blasphemy. "No,"
she admitted, "nobody was healed." Then she smiled and remarked
cheerfully, "But I am sure it did them all a lot of good."

Did it? One day, perhaps, one of those children will have the
opportunity of being healed. He may reject it. "How can a spiritual
healer help," he may ask, "when the miraculous power of the
Catholic Church at Lourdes could not?"

The following case illustrates that such a reaction is not unlikely. I was called upon recently by a harassed woman who asked
me to come and see her daughter, who was threatening to take
her life. In a real emergency, I drop everything and go. The daughter turned out to be a married woman of a little under thirty. She
was happily married, had two delightful small children and lived
in a pleasant modern house in a village near my home. She was a
tall, thin, highly-strung girl who had suffered for four years with
a dislocated vertebrae at the top of the spine. A surgical collar
helped relieve the discomfort, pain-killers made it almost tolerable
and tranquillisers kept her happy. That was the theory. In fact,
I found her in great pain, emotionally disturbed, without hope,
and contemplating suicide.

She asked me what I thought I could do. When I told her I was a spiritual healer, she said, "You cannot possibly help me. The parish priest held a healing service in this very house for me and I was no better." I could not tell her the parish priest was a charming theologian with no more healing ability than the local butcher.

Yes, she was healed—but not completely. There is a psychic block which will not be removed until she learns to forget her religious prejudices. But she is young. She can hope.

CHAPTER FOURTEEN

DO NOT HOLD BACK

I READ a lot. I always have done. When I was a boy, I generally had an adventure story hidden in one of my school books. Today, I travel fairly regularly. Modern travel is comfortable but unexciting. But it does give me time to read.

As an Englishman, I have the natural reticence of my kind. This extends to not wanting people to know what I am reading. To confuse and confound the curious, I used to keep two boldly-lettered book covers. Whether I was reading a who-dunnit or something more erudite, I used whatever cover fitted. One was titled *The Binary System in Nuclear Algebra*, the other *Neuro-Surgery for the Handyman*.

It was interesting to see the reaction of the people sitting opposite when they finally succeeded in deciphering the title. The algebra one generally produced the same result: a sigh, a look of puzzlement, and then deep respect for the genius reading it. But the neuro-surgery cover was my favourite. The reactions it produced were amazement and incredulity followed by a dream-state as they tried to work out how anybody could use a Black-and-Decker power drill to cut through the bone structure of the human cranium. Nobody ever asked me if I was enjoying my book.

Reticence is a national characteristic. We tend to keep ourselves to ourselves. The result is introspection. This is not a healthy state. I am not suggesting that we should suddenly become extroverts, beat our wives and get raging drunk every Saturday night. Yet if we did more often make use of the safety valves nature has provided, we should be healthier. What are these safety valves?

A good cry has enormous therapeutic value. The stiff upper-lip is an anachronism. Be rigid and resist, and one day you may break. Be like a bamboo—bend, give with the wind: then you will not break. You will survive. Englishmen do not cry; nor do many of their women. They should. A good cry is nature's surest safety valve. Afterwards, your tensions disappear and you feel much better.

Anger may be one of the seven deadly sins, but an explosion of wrath is also excellent therapy. Providing you harm no one, it gives immediate relief to tension. Go to some desolate place where you are certain to be unseen and unheard. Loosen your tie. Take off your coat. Stride up and down, shouting and ranting, for ten minutes. You will quickly feel a lot better. You may even feel a little silly as you realise that the thing that is upsetting you is trivial. Or you may suddenly see the other side's point of view with a clarity your anger hid.

Learn to talk over your problems with somebody. The confessional was founded on sound psychology. It has now been superseded to some degree by the analyst's couch. Both are unnecessary. But you do need a confidant to whom you can sometimes bare your thoughts.

Most people who visit me for healing present me with their symptoms. It takes time for me to unravel the real cause of their sickness. The man with migraine, for instance, had become impotent. He felt guilt towards his wife. But initially he asked for healing for migraine. I found out about his impotency two visits later; and later still, I learned something of the reasons for that. Then there was the woman with the arthritic hip who was excessively overweight. Her arthritis was aggravated by continual worrying about her quite normal children. The obesity was the result of compulsive eating, from the same cause.

They troop in procession through my door, displaying the aches and pains openly but hiding the real causes. A true diagnosis too often reveals a foundation of introversion, frustration, doubt and ignorance. They are turned inwards—hiding their real thoughts, and letting imagined wrongs, worries and fears run riot.

Everyone has three sources of help freely available: spiritual philosophy; the guidance of those in the next world who can penetrate this world; and the brotherhood of one's fellows.

As we progress in education and in our reasoning ability, we can no longer accept the fables and fairy tales of the old religions. It is right to reject them; but the pity is that, in doing so, we tend to reject the great truths they contain. Throughout each of the world religions runs this golden thread of truth. It must be so. They all stem from the same source.

It is not for me to convert you to one religion or divert you from another. Whoever you are, wherever you are, there is probably at this moment a religious book within reach of your hand. It may be filled with superstitions and taboos. Ignore them. Look, instead, for the basic philosophy. It is there.

If you need personal help, then ask your spirit guides for it. Yes, you have guides. Later in this book I shall tell you about them. For the moment, let me tell you how to become aware of them.

Try an experiment. This evening, before you go to bed, try a "quiet moment". Undress, or loosen your clothing. Remove your shoes. Sit in a comfortable chair in a dimly lit, quiet room where you are sure of not being interrupted. It should be dim because light stimulates, as does noise, and you want to be tranquil. In this environment, cross your ankles and loosely link your hands. And in this relaxing posture, close your eyes. Let your eyeballs drift gently upwards. Clear your mind.

It is difficult, to begin with, not to think. If you find thoughts intruding, concentrate on something in your mind's eye that is unrelated to your daily life. A flower does very well.

When you are thus relaxed, speak your problem quietly as if to a friend. Do not ask for any material thing. Merely state the problem and ask for guidance in dealing with it.

After a while, you may drift off into a light doze. When you awake, you will be refreshed.

Repeat this every evening. Do not make a set routine of it. The time and place are immaterial—only the atmosphere of serenity and reception matters. One morning, soon afterwards, you will wake with the answer to your problem firmly outlined in your mind. Or one day the problem will just disappear. Or somebody will come to you out of the blue with an alternative of which you had not known. You are being helped.

Most people are shy and reluctant to ask their family or friends for help. Yet you will find that, once you have asked, those seemingly reticent folk are only too anxious to respond. You should learn to give your friends, your family and your neighbours more opportunities to help you. Do not tell them what to do. Just state your problem and ask them to aid you. You will be amazed at the result.

It was in the Book of Proverbs that I read "A man that hath friends must show himself friendly: and there is a friend that sticketh closer than a brother."

I am glad that I have now thrown those two book covers away.

The nursing-sister sounded desperate on the telephone. Her professional calm had deserted her. It was not a stranger that was seriously ill. It was her husband. He had been admitted to Cuckfield General Hospital with a fatal lung disease. He was in an oxygen tent and failing fast. Would I please heal him . . .

A spiritual healer is in a difficult position with regard to hospitals. Most hospital management committees will permit a healer to treat in-patients providing the patient requests it and the supervising physician agrees. The British Medical Council, which controls all registered medical practitioners in the United Kingdom, not only does not recognise spiritual healing but will take disciplinary action against any doctor who co-operates with a healer. I have written earlier of the complete monopoly orthodox medicine enjoys and the unfortunate result of some of its policies. In hospitals, the doctors generally adopt the attitude that if the patient is dying the healer can do no harm. They therefore permit the healer to attend, in much the same way that a priest might be allowed at the bedside to administer last rites.

That Monday evening, with the grudging consent of the supervising physician and at the specific request of the patient's wife, I was allowed to go behind the ominous screens that surrounded a bed in Cuckfield General Hospital.

There, I discovered my patient. He was middle-aged, slim, with dark hair, brown eyes and a blue face. He was propped up by pillows under a polythene tent connected to an oxygen cylinder and valve assembly. His breathing was erratic and had the desperate sound of a man literally fighting for breath. The soft brown eyes had the hurt amazement of a trapped animal. Each breath could have been his last.

I sat by the bedside, took his hand and asked for healing. It was like connecting up a completely flat battery to an electrical charging unit. His resistance was nil. I felt I was just in time.

For the next week, his wife reported daily by telephone and I gave him absent healing.

The following Monday evening, after my regular healing clinic, I drove again to the hospital. The screens were still round the bed. But the patient was sitting up. The oxygen tent was gone. A plastic tube taped to his left nostril was connected to the oxygen apparatus. His colour was sallow but near normal. And we could talk.

A week later, the screens were gone. His colour was normal. An oxygen mask lay handy by the bed in case of an emergency. He did not need to use it. Within a week, he was home.

He came to see me a few times for further healing. He was still weak and he tired easily, but he was back to a normal life.

Three years later, the man died from a quite different illness. He had stopped coming to see me. I was not called again and I learned of his passing through a chance meeting between his wife and mine. She told Jean that the last three years were the happiest they had enjoyed. The time was precious. Like a gift, she said.

It is not easy to see the pattern. Life is a jig-saw puzzle with most of the pieces missing. You have to get the best impression you can from the few pieces that are given you. From these fragments, you can try and guess at the general content of the whole picture. But often enough that guess will be wrong.

Your jig-saw pieces might fall together to show a corner of an open field. "Ah," you say, "a pastoral scene of grace and tranquillity." How could you know that the rest of the field is full of French and English troops locked in the bloody conflict of Waterloo?

Too many people are making too many guesses. Some of us have more pieces than others. But give a man the minimum necessary to represent a recognisable yet tiny part of a pattern and his mind races to guess at the whole complexity of the broad canvas.

Many years ago, a simple French girl discovered that she was a natural healer. She tried to pass on to her family and friends some benefit from her psychic powers. She was denigrated, ridiculed and suspected. But eventually, her goodness and her ability as a spiritual healer was appreciated. Her name was Bernadette. She lived near Lourdes.

In a spiritually informed society, her natural gift might have been understood and her ability to serve her fellows appreciated. Unfortunately, she lived at a time when spiritual awareness was a crime and conformity to an artificial and superstitious dogma was the only road to piety. For on the simple foundation of one natural healer has been built the fantastic circus at Lourdes. Today, it boasts organised air and coach tours, curio and souvenir shops, hotels, statues, models, advertising, commercial exploitation and a mass emotional appeal verging on hysteria. Yet the total number of people healed at Lourdes during the whole period of its life as a healing shrine is less than many spiritual healers account for in one working month.

The accurate interpretation of a spiritual event is not easy. Those who have experienced it know that the excitement of being shown a small corner of an intricate design that previously was not even known to exist is difficult to control. The only reliable re-action is to be grateful for this revelation, to be humble at having been chosen, and to regularly "report for duty", so that the pattern —or what little of it you can see—can be explained.

When you receive your revelation, know that a door has been opened. That is all that has happened. Once, you did not know that the high wall that surrounded you had a door. Now, somebody has shown it to you.

You knock and it is opened. And through this door you can see an enchanting garden. Soon a man will come to take you by the hand, to lead you gently along the path amongst the flowers. He will not be wearing a uniformed cap with "guide" written on it. But that is what he will be. And you will recognise him.

The garden is an exciting place. It is restful and relaxing, yet colourful and stimulating. But there are still wrong paths you can take. And there is even a difficult maze or two. The mazes have been laboriously wrought by man. So have the wandering by-ways that all lead to dead-ends.

And it is man who has put up notices: "No Entry"; "Keep Off the Grass"; "Trespassers Will Be Prosecuted". Ignore them. The true signs are there; but not in words. Your guide knows the way for which there is no universal guide-book.

And trespassers will be forgiven.

CHAPTER FIFTEEN

A CLASSIC CASE OF HOPE

I DO not remember my education. I know I went to school. But it is like a dream, or a book I read, or a tale about another person altogether. We did not have "O" or "A" levels in those days. But we did have something called "matriculation". And that, it seemed, was the goal of our educators. We had to pass this examination.

English was my best subject. For the English examination, we were given set books which we had to learn thoroughly. The year I sat for my matriculation, the set works were Milton's *Paradise Lost* and Shakespeare's *The Tempest*. I enjoyed the second but not the first. *Paradise Lost* rolled beautifully off the tongue, but there was so much I did not understand. Nevertheless, somewhere in the attic is a certificate confirming that I passed the English examination with distinction. To do so, I memorised long passages of Milton. Even today, some words of his will pop up in my mind. These I can then quote—to prove, I suppose, that my kind of education was not completely wasted.

This one popped up when I was trying to heal a patient:

> The mind in its own place, and in itself
> Can make a Heav'n of Hell, a Hell of Heav'n.

She was suffering from intense pain in the lower back. She had had a detailed medical examination, X-rays, and a full month under observation in hospital. They could discover nothing wrong with her. The pains were real enough, but they were generated by her emotions. She came to me for healing. After each visit, she was much better. The pain either went completely or was reduced to a dull ache. But after forty-eight hours in her home environment, the pain was back.

There was nothing physically wrong with her. She was bright

and intelligent. But she was tied to the humdrum job of house-work, shopping, cooking and bringing up the children. She wanted to mix with people and use her mind. Her husband, however, insisted that her place was in the home.

The pains in her back were her method of resenting the life she felt forced to lead. She loved her children and her husband, of course, and she had a nice home. "We are not rich, but we have enough," she said. Yet her mind was a "Hell of Heav'n".

This woman was far from unique. At least half my patients have aches and pains aggravated by their environment. The other major contributors towards their ailments are fear and guilt. Most of the old orthodox religions teach the reward-and-punishment pattern. Do good and you will be rewarded. Do bad and you will be punished.

The priesthood alone decide what is good and what is bad. They set out a rigid code of behaviour for both conduct and thought. You do see men who disregard the code, though. Some of them prosper and even seem to enjoy life. Therefore, to demonstrate the infallibility of their teachings, the priests maintain that the rewards will come after death—and so will the punishments. Be good, obey, stick to the rules, and you will be rewarded. You may even qualify for eternal life. Be bad—disregard the code—and you will inevitably reap dire punishment. You may even qualify for eternal damnation.

This is taught to young children. It is contained in the orthodox teaching in all state schools. It is regularly endorsed by suitable extracts from the Bible and from the Book of Common Prayer. Be good, my children, and you will be rewarded. Be bad, and you will receive terrible punishments after you die—and for ever and ever.

When the children grow up, they may be able to reason for themselves. They may have access to books by more enlightened philosophers. They may have their eyes opened to the facts of life after death, to their own immortality, to the natural laws of cause and effect—to the truth. But for most, there lingers deep in their mind the fear of eternal damnation, the guilt, the fear of punishment, and the inevitability of it all.

If a woman has been told that her job is in the home, that she must honour and obey her husband, and that any desires to do

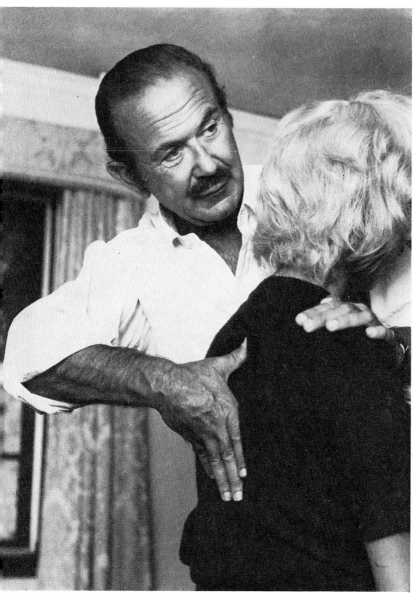

At a healing session at his home Tester treats a woman patient.

Mr. and Mrs. M. H. Tester with some of their children at the front door of The Droveway House

otherwise are evil, she then develops a guilt complex. And guilt is a killer. It creates its own particular hell. It makes her ill, not just in her mind but physically. And it can cause all the symptoms of any of a dozen major diseases.

When I find that, after one or two visits to me, a patient is not responding to healing, I question him about his environment. I often get a picture of frustration, aggravation, resentment, fear and guilt. Then I know the illness is emotionally induced. The patient's real need, in order to be healed, is philosophical re-education and spiritual reorientation.

To him, I talk of the life of the spirit. When I have pointed out the road, I recommend to him those who have travelled a long way down it, the guide-books, and the signposts. To him, I offer hope. And hope will overcome the inhibitions and threatened punishments that orthodoxy have created.

I used to hate Milton. But I kept finding little gems buried in the mass of verbiage.

> Yet when an equal poise of hope and fear
> Does arbitrate the event, my nature is
> That I incline to hope rather than fear.

And that is what I, as a Spiritualist, have to offer—hope. It is hope that will help us rise above our environment, shake off the guilt and the fear of punishment, get rid of resentment and frustration . . . hope for a future founded on knowledge and understanding in place of ignorance and superstition.

My patients educate me. Regular contact with men and women who are sick in mind and body is an experience of incalculable value. When a man visits his doctor, he expects to be given a prescription or a course of treatment that will help to cure his disease, or at least ameliorate the symptoms. A patient calling on a healer has the same attitude. He hopes to be made a little better. He expects only to have the pain eased or the distressing symptoms made more bearable.

This attitude is one that merges as a result of previous ex-perience with orthodox medicine. But why should a patient accept a palliative? Why not expect robust, bounding good health?

Good health is the natural condition of life on earth. Anything else is abnormal. Like many other abnormalities, bad health is the

G

result of perversion. We live according to simple natural laws: break these laws and the result is unhappiness and illness.

Sickness and suffering are not the work of God. They are the creations of man. Yet we have become so used to seeing them in our daily environment that we now accept them as both natural and normal.

Nearly all babies are born with the ability and the physical equipment to lead full, happy and healthy lives. Yet even at (or before) the moment of birth, babies are being physiologically perverted. Thalidomide is one terrible example of the effect on children of a drug their mothers took during pregnancy. This tragedy has rightly achieved wide publicity.

But other perversions are apparently accepted without comment. Take the case of a mother who refuses to breast-feed her baby. The grounds for doing so may seem justified. She may find it socially inconvenient. She may wish to preserve her figure. She may think up a number of excuses for her selfishness. And so the baby is fed on the milk of a cow. The cow has been fed on grass treated with insecticides and may have a high radioactive absorption. Or the cow may have been treated with hormones or given massive doses of other drugs to increase the milk yield. How many potentially harmful chemicals the baby digests at this critical stage in its growth is difficult to assess.

From babyhood onward, our diet is degraded. We eat meat years old from cold stores. It has been thawed, dyed and chemically treated to make it seem fresh, red and tender. The animal from which the meat was hacked was probably the product of intensive breeding. It had, no doubt, been treated with drugs and chemicals to promote quick growth. How much of these chemicals gets into your body?

Our bread is made white with chalk. Most of the natural nutriment is removed in the interest of easy manufacture and facile sales promotion. Our food is processed, treated with dyes, chemicals and artificial flavouring, dehydrated and quick frozen. Twentieth-century-man gives more consideration to the quality of the fuel he puts into his car than to the food he puts into his stomach.

Abounding good health is a natural state. To achieve and maintain it, we need to feed our bodies a natural diet; to provide them with fresh air, exercise and sunshine; to keep them clean—but otherwise, to think of them as little as possible. Too much care of and over-concern for your body is a certain overture to sickness.

Do not dwell on your physical condition. Do not talk about sickness and disease. Be positive, not negative. Talk, instead, of health and well-being. Think it, too.

Like produces like. Think and talk about health and happiness and you will become healthy and happy. Think and talk about unhappiness and disease and you will become miserable and ill. Every bad or negative thought breeds others. Hatred, anger, jealousy, malice, avarice and revenge all have children. They are misery, sickness, ill-health, pessimism, failure and despondency. The health of your body, like the health of your mind, depends on your attitude to living.

The time must surely come when preventive medicine is universally practised. The doctor's job will be not to heal bodies but to treat attitudes of the mind. A healthy mind—thinking good, positive and optimistic thoughts—will produce a healthy body. The true physician is a teacher. His real job must be to keep people well: to prevent illness rather than to cure it.

We already have adequate knowledge. In the recorded teaching of a hundred philosophers, in the observations of a thousand physicians, we now have the knowledge. What we lack is the determination to apply it. Let us start with our children.

Let us teach our children to abolish all the taboos of death, all thoughts of sickness, all bad emotions—like hatred, malice, envy and intolerance. Let us produce a generation that thinks positive thoughts, not negative ones; who are optimists, not pessimists; who live in harmony with natural laws and who reject any form of disharmony.

Let our children grow up *knowing* that full, abounding good health and happiness are their natural heritage. And in every home let there be inscribed, where those who dwell there can daily see them, the words "God is well, and so are you".

CHAPTER SIXTEEN

QUESTIONS! QUESTIONS!

MOST people who come to me for healing are in a muddle. Their thinking process is far from clear. Their emotions are inhibited. Their spiritual education is distorted by the indoctrination of orthodoxy. When they are healed, they ask questions. I try to answer them. Some questions are original: most are not. Here are the ones I am asked most often, and the replies I give.

Why should this happen to me?

You will persist in regarding adversity as a punishment. It is not. Sometimes, it is the result of a self-induced cause. If you have little or no faith, you will worry and fret. This could produce an ulcer. To what extent the ulcer is a punishment for your lack of faith depends only on how you look at it. You could say it was the direct result of your ignorance and poor attitudes: for most of your problems are self-induced. The others are a test. How you deal with them is the measure of your spiritual progress.

Earlier, I quoted Aughey. It is a quotation I often use to my patients. Perhaps I may be excused for repeating it here:

> God brings men into deep waters not to
> drown them but to cleanse them.

Cheer up. The mere fact that you are asking these questions shows that you are at last seeking the truth. You will find it, eventually.

Is it wrong to lose my temper?

Anger is one of the seven deadly sins—deadly to you. When you get angry, adrenalin is pumped into your bloodstream. Your pulse rate goes up, your blood pressure goes up, your blood clotting rate goes up—and one day you, too, may go up, with a thrombosis or a haemorrhage.

Lose your temper and you lose control of your destiny. You lose your friends. You could lose your health and even your earthly life. The price of anger is too high.

Should I become a vegetarian?

We are superior to animals. We have a trusteeship for them. It is wrong to exploit them for our personal benefit. This I believe. It follows that I cannot condone hunting them, experimenting on them, farming them, or eating them.

If you feel as I feel, you must become a vegetarian. If you do not, then perhaps you will when you have developed spiritually a little further. If you are uncertain, I suggest you arrange a visit to a slaughterhouse when it is busy. Afterwards, you should have no doubts.

Do you believe in God?

Yes. Wherever I look, I can see portions of an extremely intricate design. I cannot see it all. I probably never will. But the little I can see is wonderful. When there is a design, there must be a designer. You can call him God or Allah or the Great White Spirit or the Life Force.

I agree with Swift:

> That the universe was formed
> by a fortuitous concourse of
> atoms, I will no more believe
> than that the accidental jumbling
> of the alphabet would fall into
> a most ingenious treatise of
> philosophy.

Should I worry?

No. The extent of your worry is the measure of your lack of faith. Worry clouds the mind, lowers your body's efficiency, and creates an atmosphere of doubt and unhappiness. You sleep badly, wake unrefreshed, and infect those around you.

Think out your problems, analyse them, do your level best, and then stop. You can do no more. Let those who guide you take over and do the rest.

What charities should I support?

Organised charities are far from being an unqualified blessing. Those who join committees and arrange concerts, balls and raffles do much good, I am sure; but their very organising ability excuses thousands the need to do good personally.

Give to whatever charity moves you. But always remember that this is nothing like enough. Charity should be an important part of your working philosophy—a regular facet of your daily life. Many know the recommendation in Acts 20: "It is more blessed to give than to receive." What they forget is that you have to give yourself, too.

Is drinking wrong?

Alcohol is a drug. Do not be diverted by the advertising or by the ease with which it can be obtained. It is a drug and it can be addictive. If you can manage to go through life without it, you will be all the better for this discipline. If you cannot, be sure that you control it and that it does not control you. Tranquillity, relaxation and a sense of well-being are the natural results of a spiritual exercise. This is the only true way. Drugs, chemicals and alcohol are perversions.

Should I give up smoking?

Yes, if you can.

It is an odd list of questions but, as I have said, these are the ones I am asked most often. Few patients ask about immortality, fewer still about the source of the healing power. The advice I give seldom varies. (I must remember to read this again in twenty years time to see if I still agree with it.)

How does healing work? Where does the healing power come from? These are the questions patients should ask.

There are two kinds of healing, and it is difficult to label them. Because of the need to do so, however, I call them "Magnetic Healing" and "Spiritual Healing".

Magnetic healing is the more common of the two. You have probably met it many times. It is normally a gift that is enjoyed by a man of strong personality—an optimist. He exudes confidence, strength and faith in the future. Around such a man is an aura of power. If you are feeling depressed, run down or ill, contact with his magnetic personality lifts you up and makes you feel so much better. In fact, you take some of his power and use it. To some degree, this depletes him. After helping a number of people in this way, the healer feels tired. He has given some of his stock of power to others. He needs to rest and restore himself.

This power is not restricted to healers. It is shown in different ways. The groom who can control a nervous thoroughbred; the nurse who walks a restless ward at night, saying a word here and straightening a pillow there, and leaving tranquillity in her wake; the schoolteacher who enters a classroom of unruly youngsters and, within a few moments, has their full attention; the doctor who sits at a bedside and, without any treatment, leaves the patient feeling much better; the gardener for whom plants grow particularly well; the friend to whom you turn for help and who says little but somehow lightens your burden . . . They all have the same power.

Positive thinking, optimism and faith generate this aura. It affects animals, people, plants and even seemingly fortuitous events. When you meet a man with such power, you adopt for a while the positive virtues that clothe him. And they work for your good. Thus you are lifted up, the natural harmony of your body is restored and you feel physically so much better.

This, then, is magnetic healing. The faith healer relies on it heavily. He is a man of strong personality. He knows the body is a self-healing mechanism. If he can convince you of your ability to get well, you can heal yourself of many ailments. He uses his personality, first to make you feel better and then to convince you that the improvement can be maintained. If you are convinced, you generate faith in your recovery. This faith is powerful. It will improve or cure psychosomatic illness. The faith healer succeeds by the sheer strength of his personality, by the faith he uncovers in you, and by the emotional environment he uses as a hot-bed for the forced growth of his power.

I am not a faith healer. Nor do I practise magnetic healing. Some find my philosophy helpful; others say that they feel so much better when they are coming to see me, even before we meet.

I seldom talk about the philosophy until after healing has taken place. The aura I generate is there, but I do not rely on it for healing. It may condition a patient to become more receptive, but that is all. My healing is of the second type. It is spiritual healing.

There is, around us, an enormous power which I will label "the Life Force". This is not an original title. George Bernard Shaw used it, and it will suffice. This is the power that brings out the leaves and the flowers every spring; controls the seasons; makes the crops and the fruits grow and ripen; gives energy to a baby, and grows and strengthens it into a man. The force can be seen in action everywhere we look. It operates in each of us.

Those who are ill need this force to be focused on their bodies in general and on their ailments in particular. To concentrate the power, you need an instrument. It has to pick up the power, change the vibration or wavelength to one the sick person can assimilate, and concentrate it on that one body—or on one particular organ or joint in that body.

The instrument is not a machine. It is a man. He has been given the gift of receiving the power of the Life Force and transforming it into a concentrated vibration that heals. The gift is not one that many enjoy. Those who have it must develop it. A healer does an important task. To do it well, he needs help.

There are those in the spirit world who wish to spend some time helping us here. They do this because it aids their own spiritual development and because of a genuine love of humanity. To this end, they seek a man in this world who has the psychic faculty that is needed. He is, in fact, earmarked as a healer before his life here commences. The spirit helpers, or guides, watch and aid his development. A healer needs to know suffering and compassion. He needs to have lived a full life. When he is ready, the healing gift is developed.

It is sometimes wrong to heal a particular ailment unless the body will sustain the improvement; and many of those who visit me are very run down. Often, the sickness is merely symptomatic of a generally poor physical condition. For these patients, a different procedure is used by the guides. They note the particular sickness but they disregard it for the time being. The healing force is not concentrated but is generalised. This results in a general "toning up" of the body. The metabolism is restored to normal and the sick person becomes more in harmony with his environment. I can often see this healing tonic at work. Then, after a few visits, when the patient's general health is improved, the guides concentrate briefly on the particular disease that brought him to me. And the ailment is healed.

The faith healer works hard to generate the emotional environment in which the sick can heal themselves. He uses many aids to create the right atmosphere. These may include a sanctuary of an ecclesiastical nature, incense, tall wax candles, sacred music, rituals, "magic" passes, and clothing of a mystical nature.

I shun them all. I heal in a bright room in my shirtsleeves. There is no special place where healing is better than in any other. I could heal a man in a public convenience if he asked to be healed and was ready to receive it.

The healing that flows through me comes from without. I am just an instrument. It takes nothing from me. Rather, it leaves a little as it passes. At the end of a healing day, when I may have treated twenty patients, I am not at all tired. In fact, I feel refreshed. And I enjoy radiant good health.

CHAPTER SEVENTEEN

CASE HISTORY

HE was a clerk in a government department—an occupation that seems undemanding. Yet he was a perfectionist. And most perfectionists are sad. Perfection is not meant to be our lot. We do the best we can, but nature's work will always be superior. We strive, yet we know we must compromise. In the end, whatever we do is transitory. No painting man has created can compare with a sunset, no object of virtue with a snowflake, no feat of engineering with the construction of the human body.

His only relaxation was ballroom dancing. The dance floor knows no class distinction. There he felt an equal to his fellows as, with his wife as a partner, he glided to soft music into the escapist world of the waltz.

His continual worry about his work made him ill. As a result, he developed an ulcer. The orthodox medical treatment was to operate and remove it. He went into hospital, had the operation and was discharged. The demand for beds was so heavy, he was discharged prematurely. There was no money for a holiday or for a long convalescence. He returned to work.

A few days later, he suddenly became giddy when descending a flight of stone steps. He fell and broke his ankle.

On readmission to hospital, the X-rays disclosed a severe fracture. He was in plaster for some weeks. When the plaster was eventually removed, he was sent home.

Two weeks later, a routine check by his doctor disclosed that the fracture had not set cleanly. He was again admitted to the hospital. In the operating theatre, the ankle was rebroken and a steel pin was inserted in the bone.

When he returned to work, some weeks later, he was still in pain and limping. His work was behindhand and he had to put in overtime most nights. The ankle continued to give him pain and the limp became worse. He used a stick and walked with an odd twisting gait.

Within a month, he had developed sciatic twinges in his leg and an intense pain in his back. He reported back to the hospital outpatients department. The orthopaedic surgeon X-rayed his back and reported he had dislocated a lumbar vertebrae. They put him in a surgical corset.

Limping still, his ankle swollen and inflamed, wearing an orthopaedic jacket from chest to hip, with pain in his back and periodic agony in his leg, he tried to carry on. Not unnaturally, his work suffered. It became ragged and he got more behindhand. He found himself becoming sick, with a low tolerance to certain foods. After a particularly severe bout of vomiting, he consulted his doctor—only to hear the diagnosis he dreaded. He had another ulcer.

He felt like taking his life. He could no longer tolerate the pain, the discomfort, the sheer inevitability of being ill for the rest of his days. Then a friend who had heard of my healing told him about me, and he came to see me in London.

It took a long time for him to tell me this sorry tale. I listened with compassion. When I was sure I had the full picture, I laid my hands on his shoulders and sought attunement.

Where to begin? When a patient has a number of ailments linked by circumstances or some form of apparent cross-infection, I do not initially try to heal any particular symptom.

My hands rested lightly on his shoulders. As if by its own volition, my right hand moved to his stomach and began to vibrate deeply. Then his shoulders and his spine received attention. He was very run down.

There is a sort of automatic demand valve in the healing circuit. Patients receive what they need. This man had been nearly emptied of the life force. He required replenishing. I felt the healing power flowing strongly through me.

It took three sessions before he was strong enough. Then the healing became more concentrated. I dealt at each appointment with the ulcer, the ankle, the vertebrae and the sciatica. And each week I could see some progress as his body became stronger and the defects were remedied.

At the end of about three months, his ulcer had dispersed and he was eating well. The sciatica had gone and, apart from some minor cramp at night, his leg was free of pain. The ankle-swelling had gone down and, although he felt insecure at times, he walked with no limp and had discarded the stick. The vertebrae had returned to its normal position and his back was free of pain and fully flexible.

This was the moment to start him on the path of philosophical re-education. I talked to him about life, about his own immortality, about a design for living and a pattern of thinking. I lent him books to read. He began to stop worrying and to start living.

I have written in some detail of this particular case in order to dispel the picture of miraculous instant healing that some people imagine always happens. There are many cures that are immediate and spontaneous. Men and women have been carried into my room and have walked out ten minutes later. But often, the process of healing is slow and methodical. It requires application by both healer and patient. Healing is a natural process. Sometimes, nature's rate may seem slow. A healer learns to recognise the rate and adjust to it.

It would have been exciting to have been able to wave a magic wand and see that man healed before my very eyes in a flash of heavenly light. Yet it was just as rewarding when one afternoon he greeted me warmly with the words, "Yesterday evening, my wife and I did two full circuits of the ballroom in a slow waltz."

Every patient has a different tale to tell. There are great variations in the symptoms of the most common incurable diseases. Each person that comes to me for healing is too complex for me to understand fully. Each has had an individual experience in religious training, academic education, personal relationships and environmental conditioning. Fully to appreciate all their complexes would need months of research and analysis.

As a practising healer, I do not have the time or the experience or even the opportunity to do this. Fortunately, I do not have to. There is a common denominator in all healing. It operates at two levels. First, by contact healing, I stop or greatly reduce the actual pain. Then I bring the patient into harmony. It is difficult to explain this process. Let me give you an example.

Suddenly, you are awake. The illuminated clock by the side of your bed tells you it is 3 a.m. Some moonlight seeps through the curtains. It is bright enough for you to see a dark figure crouching in the far corner of the room. It is menacing you with a gun.

Your throat is dry. You want to shout out; to scream; to cry for help. But you cannot. Adrenalin is pumping into your bloodstream. Your heart pounds away as your pulse rate soars. Your blood pressure goes up. Your head feels as though it will burst. All the defence mechanisms of your body are alerted. Your blood increases its ability to clot, in case you are wounded. You are damp with perspiration.

Slowly, your hand creeps towards the bedside light switch. Your eyes never leave the black, crouching, menacing figure in the corner. Your questing fingers find the smooth plastic surface. You press down the button. The room is flooded with light.

The corner is occupied only by a chair. It is made bulky and unrecognisable by the dark coat you threw over it when you came in late last night. The umbrella you brought into the room, unthinkingly hooked over your arm, projects from it like the barrel of a gun.

You give a nervous laugh, then a great release of breath as the tension leaves you. A drink of water, a small adjustment of your pillows and you are soon fast asleep again.

In a few minutes, the mechanism of your body has gone from the quiet tick-over of sleep to the roaring awareness of danger and then back again. During this whole period, you were sitting up in bed. There was no physical activity. Yet you might equally have just run a mile or finished Round One of a boxing match.

What triggered off your body's defence mechanism was your attitude. And it was your attitude that told the defences to "stand down" once the danger had passed.

You cannot directly control this mechanism. If you find your fist balled to punch a man in the face, you can give it a direct command to unclench. If the command is clear and calm, your hand will respond.

You have no such control over your body's defences. You cannot directly control the quantities of adrenalin in your bloodstream, the clotting ability of your blood, your pulse rate, or your blood pressure. These respond not to your conscious mind but to your attitudes.

If, when you awoke in the early hours, you had recognised the bulk in the corner of the room as a chair, an overcoat and an umbrella, then your body would have remained normal. You would have made yourself comfortable and gone back to sleep. The whole sequence of events that followed was the result of your attitude—apprehension, fear, danger.

The example I have given is, perhaps, an extreme one. Let us therefore look at something more commonplace.

A businessman sits at his desk, reading the morning's correspondence. He knows his appointment book is full and that he has a tiring and frustrating day ahead of him. He picks up a letter and reads it. A firm on whose business he was depending writes to repudiate a big order. He is furious.

"Who do they think they are! They can't get away with this. I'll show them. Miss Jones, take a letter."

His attitude triggers off the whole defence mechanism of his body. Heart, pulse, blood pressure, blood clotting ability—they are all working to defend him from the enemy his aggressive attitude indicates. Perhaps he has second thoughts, takes a drink of cold water, cools down a little and decides to think it out rather than to leap into action. The body records the altered attitude and readjusts to normalcy.

One day, perhaps, this businessman meets a situation in which he is a little more upset than usual. Perhaps agitation, annoyance, bursts of temper and aggression have become part of his daily business routine. On this day, his blood increases its clotting ability on his mental danger signal and then fails to revert to normal. A real clot is formed. The man dies of thrombosis. Or a blood vessel overworked by constant changes in pressure gives way and the body dies of a haemorrhage.

Your body is constantly manufacturing chemicals and secretions. These it maintains at the correct balance for you to enjoy health and well-being. It varies the balance to adjust to circumstances and environment—from the quiet tick-over of sleep to the roaring awareness of danger.

Most of the diseases we have are caused by our body mechanisms being overworked, confused or just abused. They are constantly triggered off by wrong attitudes.

Over fifty per cent of all patients referred to hospitals for treatment are suffering from ailments that are emotionally induced. This means that if a medical student opened a textbook of the thousand most common diseases, he would find that emotionally-induced illness was more prevalent than all the nine hundred and ninety-nine others put together.

Among a few of the complaints that have been found to be emotionally induced are pains in the neck, lumps in the throat, ulcers, gall-bladder pains, gas in the stomach, dizziness, constipation, tiredness, arthritis, headaches, backaches, sciatica, defective vision, fibrositis, lack of appetite and obesity. But if your illness is emotionally induced, it does not hurt any less. The pain and discomfort are real enough. You do not imagine your illness. It exists.

To maintain a balance in your body's functions, you must control your attitude to life itself. To do so, you need to adopt a well-tried spiritual philosophy. Once I have helped a patient to become free of pain, or of other disturbing symptoms, it becomes my duty to introduce him to such a philosophy. Thus, he can dictate his daily attitudes. Through that philosophy, his body can become in harmony. The imbalances are adjusted. He enjoys radiant health.

On such a philosophy, you too can rebuild your life. Your mundane problems will take on a new perspective. You can rise high above them. In place of fear, anger, resentment, material gain, lust and greed, you fill your mind with love, happiness, understanding and spiritual values. Your daily attitudes are tranquillity, peace and helpfulness. Your body is in harmony with your attitudes. You conquer illness because you leave room in your mind only for those emotions that induce health.

> Two men look out through the same bars:
> One sees mud and one the stars.

To what extent is it necessary for a patient to have faith to be healed? This is an important question. Many of the sick who visit me are anxious to assure me that they believe I can heal them. But this is often a belief assumed for the moment because they think it will help. Or else it is the temporary magnification of a little faith into something much bigger. I tell them not to concern themselves with the forced growth of faith. I explain that the mere fact that they have made the journey to see me and have asked for healing is enough. When I have relaxed them, I ask them to receive the healing forces without any misconception or prejudices.

Sick people enjoy varying capacities to accept healing. Each individual is at a different stage of spiritual evolvement. Each has a different degree of illness and needs a different amount and quality of healing.

Those who are already in possession of spiritual awareness accept healing as the natural process it is. They visit a healer for normal minor ailments and these are cleared up quickly.

On the other end of the scale is the man with no spiritual awareness who visits a healer as one more experience in a long series of unorthodox treatments. He is often the victim of his own wrong thinking and wrong living. His ailment is the result of this and of the unhealthy environment in which he lives. He may respond to healing, but he may not. His attitude of "I'll try anything once" is not conducive to the spiritual reorientation he really needs. He regards me in much the same light as he would a witch doctor, a voodoo expert or a practitioner in acupuncture. But such a person is the exception.

I stick firmly to the title "spiritual healer" because I want people to appreciate that a visit to me is meant to be a spiritual experience. After you have healed your first hundred patients, you get to know the true seekers after health. Those who come out of curiosity are not excluded from this group. But there is a lunatic fringe that is merely seeking new experiences, and those who come from it I convert or discourage.

Spiritual healing is not an end in itself. It is a means. When a man is healed, he is spiritually reorientated. He is swung round and left facing a road he never knew existed. This broad highway of knowledge and awareness leads him through his life here and confidently on towards the next world.

One day you, too, will face the great change we call death. I have written about how I was healed and what happened to me. I have told you of those who come to me for healing and what happened to them.

You are now coming to what is perhaps the most important part of this book—*when it happens to you.*

CHAPTER EIGHTEEN

WHAT AM I?

SOME years ago, I wrote a magazine article under the title "The Bewildered Man's Guide to Death". The editor of the magazine became tired of supplying reprints, so he reproduced it in booklet form. It received some recognition, appeared in an American publication and is still in demand. The reason for the success of this short treatise is not difficult to understand. We have a habit of saying "If I should die"; but, in our hearts, we know this is a form of evasion. We should say "When I die", because we know it happens to the best of us. Yet there is remarkably little authoritative literature on the subject.

If you were to visit a large reference library and ask the librarian to show you some books on gynaecology, you would probably find a whole wall or two devoted to the subject of being born. Apart from the medical books and textbooks, there have been a great number of volumes published for the layman (or, rather, the laywoman) on childbirth. Also available are lectures, clinics, working models, instructional films and even television programmes. Birth has its authorities, its orthodoxies and its cranks. It is fair to say that the process of being born has been remarkably well documented.

Once you are born, you can find even more written and visual aids to the science of living. There are thousands of books on your physiological needs. These include advice on diet, exercise, and general care of the body. If you want to know how to slim, or develop a large bust, or have a satisfactory sex life, you can be sure of finding a book to tell you about it.

Your philosophical needs are equally well met. In fact, the last decade has seen a great outpouring of books on how to live, how to be happy and how to become rich. It is indeed remarkable that this generation, which seems intent on destroying the world or reducing it to a place of sheer materialism and hedonism, should have access to so much disregarded advice.

Books on how to live have been with us since writing was invented. Those classified as "philosophy" have generally been erudite tomes reserved for the theologian or the scholar. But there have been others. Parts of the Bible contain a design for living, with many examples and parables to explain it. There was a time when it was regularly used as a guide to behaviour, interpreted by the priest or the head of the family.

It is easy, as you can see, to obtain all the information you need on how to be born and on how to live after that. But there are no books on how to die.

Men have written on this subject, of course. But all the books fall into one of two categories. Most of the more poetical writers concern themselves not with how to die but with the regret of dying: they are really writing about life when one is aware of its termination. In the second category are the theologians. They are on a roundabout as they try out their theories against the accepted teachings of some orthodoxy. Since most religions—especially in the West—have depended heavily on the reward-and-punishment syndrome, they have to accept a premise which is false. A theologian has to assume that it is true that if you do good you will be rewarded and if you do bad you will be punished. He can see people doing good according to the orthodox rules and yet dying in poverty. He can see others behaving badly and getting rich and obviously having fun. He must therefore qualify his doctrine. The reward and the punishment are not given in this world but in the next. Be good and you will be rewarded in heaven *after you die*. Be bad and you will be punished in hell.

It is apparent that no intelligent book on death could emerge if its author was conditioned by this doctrine. He could not see life after death except in its relationship to reward and punishment— heaven and hell. His theology is merely a mental exercise based on a false premise. No wonder there has been so much confusion about death.

There is another factor. I have always found that when I read a book by a man who knows his subject, it is written in simple words and to the point. It is easy to read and to understand. But when I read one by an ill-informed theorist, I find he uses long words—some of which are incomprehensible. He creates a vocabulary all his own, so that many of the words I do recognise have a different meaning. After reading such a book, I am confused and less clear in my mind than when I started it.

The real reason why there are no authoritative books on how to die is that the people who have written them have never died themselves. Their information is either assumed or imaginary. Or they have taken the academic musings of some theologian and permutated the possibilities.

Naturally, the average man is bewildered. As he gets older and his death draws nearer, the subject begins to assume greater importance. He starts thinking of insurance. He goes to church. He donates more to organised charity. He tries to change himself into a benign patriarch. This is all done in the hope that the first sixty years—when he was selfish, materialistic and greedy—will be forgotten in the golden glow of his old age, when he gave away some of his ill-gained wealth. "It would have gone in death duties anyway, old chap."

An insurance broker once said he could understand why so many seemingly well-educated and unsuperstitious men asked a Catholic priest to their deathbed. It does not take long to be baptised, to be accepted into the church, to confess your sins and to receive extreme unction. It costs next to nothing, yet it enables the priest to promise you an entry into heaven. "It must be the cheapest form of insurance there is," the broker remarked.

It is time the bewildered man had guidance on dying. What follows contains such guidance. It is written by an authority who has himself died a number of times before. What I write is uncluttered by any wild or outdated religious theories. I shall try and cut through the theorising, the superstitions and the pagan concepts of orthodox religious taboos.

Dying is just as important as living—and it is going to happen to YOU. You can read a guide to Iceland and never go there. You can read a treatise on space travel and never leave the ground. You can read a book on marriage and stay single all your life. But when you read a guide to death, then you know your money has not been wasted.

The first thing you must do is put aside, firmly and for all time, the childish teaching that inhibits your reasoning. Try to drain your mind of everything you have been taught about death. Forget heaven and hell. Cleanse your thoughts of the alternatives of the boredom of being waited on hand and foot by platonic houris while you indolently twang your harp or of being tormented and toasted by devils with long forks. Forget the day of judgment. There is no big book in which every good and bad deed is recorded.

Let us pretend you have never considered the subject of death before. Go back to a time before you assimilated any man-made misconceptions, to when you were a baby. Let us start at the very beginning. When you were born? Before that. When you were conceived? Before that . . .

What are you? Is your body you? No. You know it is not. Your body is an interesting mechanism. But it is merely a vehicle. It walks and talks and sings and drives a car. But it needs motivation and control to make it do all these things. This is provided by your mind. Is your mind you? No. It is not. Your mind motivates your body. It is the control room of a complex piece of equipment.

Your brain is the computer that works things out. It is part of your body's equipment. It is an intricate part and perhaps the most important. You can look at a brain in a glass jar at any medical school. Brains are, after all, just another part of the body. Butchers sell them. Some people eat them.

There is a third ingredient that has to be added to your mind and to your body to make up you. That ingredient is your spirit. Your spirit is you. Your mind and your body clothe your spirit when it is on earth.

Prove it, you say. Show me a spirit. I can see a man. Remove his clothing and I can see his body. Drill a hole in his head and I can see his brain. Show me his spirit.

Have you ever seen a dead body? You can remove the clothing. You can dissect it, including the brain. But it is not a person. It is just a carcass—a mass of flesh, bone and tissue that will quickly rot and become putrescent. It has to be shovelled underground, into a hole, or burnt like rubbish in an incinerator before it becomes too rotten.

Is this a man? A man who lived, loved, composed great music, wrote moving poetry, invented, imagined, theorised and romanced?

You know it is not. The one vital ingredient is missing. His spirit is no longer contained in his body. He is dead.

Be assured that in this life you are composed of three essential parts: your body, which is the vehicle you occupy for your earthly existence; your mind, which is the control mechanism of your body; and your spirit, which animates your body and your mind and gives life to the whole.

Only the mind and the body die. The spirit is indestructible. You are not a body and a mind which have a spirit. You are a spirit being expressed for the present through a temporal mind and body. The spirit is you.

CHAPTER NINETEEN

WHY AM I HERE?

THERE is another world. It is the world of spirit. You have come from it. You will return to it. It is removed from this world not in time or distance but in its wavelength. The other world exists on a different plane.

Suppose you came upon Rip Van Winkle today and he had just woken up after being asleep for a hundred years. You could say to him, "Around you there is music. Orchestras are playing symphonies. Brass bands are playing marches. There is music for dancing; people are singing; the air is full of wonderful sounds." And he would probably think you mad. Yet if you put your hand into your pocket and took out a transistor radio, you would have only to turn a switch. Then he could hear the sounds of the music that surrounded him but of which he was totally ignorant.

The spirit world is all around us, too. It is at a different vibration, on a different wavelength, on a different plane. We, too, must have a receiving set if we are to tune in to it. We do not use a piece of electronic equipment. Our apparatus is a person called a sensitive or, to some people, a medium.

Through a medium, we are able to communicate with the spirit world. We cannot call on them any more than you can call to the broadcasting studio through a radio receiver. The medium is merely a receiver. When the time and the environment are right, he can "tune in". He may be in a trance or he may be seemingly wide awake. In the state of attunement, he can receive the spirit wavelength and convert it to one we can understand. It is not so different from the transistor radio that picks up a radio signal and converts it into a vibration we can hear. This form of communication is well established. Once you are receiving from the other world, the comparison with the simple radio is no longer valid.

The medium can talk back. And from these conversations, we obtain knowledge.

We know, for instance, that all spirits are going through a continual process of refinement. As it progresses through the varying stages of evolution, a spirit feels the need of extra experience, further education, added awareness. It is in this world of ours that a spirit finds some of that experience. Life here is simply an education—and a pretty primary education at that. Your life here is chosen because it will give your spirit the experience, the suffering, the challenge and the opportunity it needs at this point in its evolution.

All of us have spiritual helpers. They are kindred souls who have chosen to aid us. They advise, comfort and help us deal with our troubles and our problems. In the other world, you will have discussed with your guides the type of education and experiences you needed to further your spiritual evolvement. You decide—and the final decision must be yours—that a period on earth in a life presenting certain challenges will provide the opportunity. It is like having a completely frank analysis of your knowledge and your psychology and deciding the course of education that will help correct the deficiencies.

Your guides visit this world. They consider all the factors. They help you choose the life that will accord with your spiritual needs. They bid their adieus to you—perhaps sorrowfully, because they know your awareness of them will be minimal for many years. You go into a deep sleep.

In this world, a man and a woman who are to be your temporal parents come together. The seed in the woman's womb is fertilised. At that moment, you—as a spirit—enter into the life of a newly conceived and as yet unborn child. The spirit enters the child at the moment of conception. There is, therefore, nothing wrong with contraception. The seed is not fertilised. Spiritual life is not begun. But once the seed has been fertilised, life is there. That is why abortion is wrong. It is the taking of life.

The child spends nine months in the warmth and comfort of its mother's womb. Then it emerges into the air for the remainder of its life. But it begins to exist as a living entity at the moment of conception. It is at that moment that the spirit leaves the other world and enters this one.

We rejoice when a child is born. We mourn when a person dies. In the spirit world it is the opposite. They are a little sad when a child is born, because it means a passing from their world. They rejoice when a person dies, because his period of education and testing here is over and he is reunited with those he loves.

People who are in pain or ill, or who have suffered a loss, sometimes say to me, "Why should this happen to me? I have always lived a good life. I have never done anybody any harm. Why should I suffer?" Your suffering is part of your education. The sword may not like being heated in the furnace, but it will be a much better sword once the steel is tempered. And you will be a better person spiritually once you have suffered and have learned to rise above it.

As a refreshing contrast to this complaining, I have heard a man thank God for having chosen him to face so many trials and tribulations. He felt honoured that he had been singled out for special consideration, that his soul was being tempered for some great work—and he felt uplifted. He knew, as you too must realise, that life on earth is an education.

The extent to which you benefit from your treatment of life's problems is the measure of your spiritual evolution and of your fitness to pass on to a higher plane.

After you are born, you have free will within certain limitations. There are many theories about free will and predestination. These two definitions have kept theologians busy for centuries. Today, we can see two extremes. At one end of the scale is the Eastern mystic. His belief is that every act and event in his life is pre-destined. "It is written." He sits cross-legged and motionless, starving, amid dirt and squalor. Nothing he does can make any difference to the preordained pattern of his life. So he does nothing.

The other extreme is the Western materialist. He is an atheist. He believes nothing. He puts material gain and personal pleasure above all things as he elbows his way up. "I'm all right, Jack."

They are both completely wrong.

Let us look at predestination first. You were born a white European, or a black Negro, or a yellow Asiatic. This you cannot change. Your height, build, colour of eyes, ethnic grouping—these you cannot change, either. Your mother and father had certain characteristics, certain strains in their genes, and these have been passed on to you.

You were born in Europe in the twentieth century. If you had wanted to be born the first son of the Doge of Venice in the sixteenth century, you could not now arrange it. You come into this world with certain prearranged characteristics and in a fixed point in temporal time. The span of your life is known. The general pattern it will take and the type and quality of the problems you will face are known. It may be a physical or mental disability, an unfaithful wife, financial difficulties, loneliness, drug addiction, alcoholism or bigamy: all the infinite permutations of the trials life here presents that will be applied to you are known.

When you, as a spirit, enter your mother's womb and take possession of the fertilised seed that is there, your memory of your earlier spiritual life is almost completely erased. During your temporal life, a part of this pre-natal memory will be allowed to penetrate your spiritual awareness. You will experience here some degree of personal revelation. This, too, is known.

Within this overall pattern, you do enjoy free will—but it is, in itself, subjected to a certain natural law. The whole of the universe depends on this law: the law of cause and effect. If you plant a daffodil bulb, comes spring and you have a tall yellow daffodil. You do not have a tulip or a sunflower. Cut yourself, and you bleed. Live a good life, eat a balanced diet, do not degrade or pollute your body or mind, and you enjoy happiness and health. Follow a reciprocal course, and the result is misery and disease. The cause and effect of the natural law is immutable.

It is a simple law. Science, philosophy, life itself—all depend on the basic law of cause and effect. This law governs your own life, too. *For every major action you take has a reaction.* The acts you do, the attitudes you adopt, the things you say are like stones tossed into a pool. The ripples spread in widening circles and meet other circles and change them.

Although our pre-natal memories are erased when we are born, some spiritual awareness remains in our subconsciousness. Every man in the course of his life here is given an opportunity to recognise some degree of personal spiritual revelation. The degree varies from person to person and depends on the extent to which one's spirit has evolved.

For instance, you may be in pain, suffering from a disease like osteo-arthritis, for which orthodox medicine has no cure. Perhaps, after years of painful discomfort, you are recommended to a spiritual healer. And you are healed. The pain and the stiffness disappear. You are straight and fit and well again. Then know that the healing has been given to you to provide you with your moment of spiritual revelation. If you then become sufficiently alert to ask questions about what really happened to you, to learn something of the healing forces that have come to your aid, to investigate the wondrous knowledge and faith and happiness that spiritual awareness brings to men, then you have your revelation.

It may be a lesser moment—one when you are suddenly made aware of the right road to take. You may be faced with a decision that, at first sight, appears purely a commercial one. The step you believe to be morally right seems to lead to financial failure; the alternative would appear to give you worldly riches but means acting against your conscience. The decision is clear-cut. A moral blunder might prevent you regaining the right road. A correct decision could open the way to spiritual progress.

It may be even simpler . . . an act of loving kindness as an alternative to one of stern, unyielding self-righteousness.

The law of cause and effect cannot be altered. It cannot be bent. It cannot be ignored. Recognise this natural law and live according to your best interpretation of it. Accept your problems as tests of your spiritual progress. Recognise the opportunities of personal revelation. Always do what is morally right even if, at the time, it seems to be commercially wrong. Remember that, within the broad framework of place, time, race and hereditary characteristics, you have free will.

Lincoln's Gettysburg address is based on a fallacy. I will not quote it all. The best known extract is:

> Fourscore and seven years ago our fathers brought forth on this continent a new nation, conceived in liberty, and dedicated to the proposition that all men are created equal.

On this statement a whole political philosophy has been established. Yet the premise is false. Each one of us is at a different stage of his spiritual evolution. Two men may appear superficially similar. But one may be an advanced being, spiritually aware and philosophically mature, and the other may be brutish, immature and in his spiritual infancy. Each has come here to lead a life that will give him the spiritual education he needs. One is almost ready to pass on to the university of the next world. The other is proving inadequate even in this kindergarten. They were not created equal.

One man has a perfect physique, another is a deformed cripple. One man composes great music, another is tone deaf. One man paints wondrously, another cannot draw a straight line. One man is a concert pianist, another cannot keep time on a toy drum. One man is psychic, another is purely materialistic.

There is no equality. Each man is the product of his environment, his hereditary genes, and the degree of spiritual education he has so far been able to assimilate.

Froude, in *Party Politics*, wrote, "Men are made by nature unequal. It is vain, therefore, to treat them as if they were equal." And he was right.

Perhaps what Lincoln really meant was that men are created with equal opportunity. But this, too, is untrue. A man in the early stages of his spiritual evolution may be born into this world with the primitive brutishness that equips him for a lowly task, such as slaughterman in an abattoir. Another comes to us to complete the final facet of his already very advanced education and, whilst here, shares a revelation that changes the destiny of a whole nation. Where is the equality?

Men are not, and never have been, created equal. The continued promotion of this fallacy only succeeds in bringing us all down to the lowest common denominator. If men are not created equal and if there is no equality of opportunity, what is left?

I have told you that we come to this world by choice. We may come here many times. Each visit is to live a life designed to further our spiritual education, to experience what we need for our evolution.

We have two handicaps. The first is ignorance. If we are here to be educated, then we must be in need of the education. Until we have it, we must be inhibited by our lack of it. The second is the limitation of the physical body we occupy for this life. It may be weak, crippled, disabled or deformed. It may be strong and lusty. It may be one of a large range of colours and sizes. It may be controlled by a mind of exquisite complexity. It may have the mind of a moron.

Our task is to make the most of what we have—spiritually, mentally and physically. No one has any other task. To this extent only do we enjoy equality.

When your life here is over, as I shall explain, you will review it. In your assessment, the only criterion you can use is the degree to which you left the world a better place—considering the tools and equipment you were given with which to do it.

This is your equality. The right to be able to say, "The world is a better place because of me." And if I remind you, in modern parlance, "It's what you do with what you've got," I am only paraphrasing what has been said many times before.

> Every man hath his proper gift
> of God, one after this
> manner, and another after that.
>   1 Corinthians.

CHAPTER TWENTY

WILL I BE PUNISHED IF I DO WRONG?

PUNISHMENT has a number of meanings. You can be punished by omission. If the other boys have ice cream and you have none, you may think this a punishment. If all the girls have boy friends except you—this, too, may seem a punishment. You can punish yourself by your own conscience: for if you do something you know to be morally wrong you can worry yourself, by remorse, into a state of serious physical illness. This is the cause and effect law I have already told you about.

A wrong action may poison your whole life. Things start going wrong for you. You are troubled, not at peace with yourself and out of harmony with nature. You may find that, in your old age, you are embittered and disillusioned. Looking back on your life, it seems empty and futile. This, too, is punishment.

If you do a right act, then you feel good. You are relaxed, warmly happy and in harmony. The people around you respond to this atmosphere. Things start going right for you. Keep it up, and you near the end of your earthly life content that it has been useful and well spent.

I have written about a right act and a wrong act. For in spite of what the modern psychiatrists say, and the ready excuses they find to justify human behaviour, there is a well-defined right and wrong. As we evolve spiritually, we become more aware of this code.

No person is infallible. But it *is* possible to know what is right in any set of circumstances. Vivisection, and the five million experiments carried out on living animals in Britain every year (eighty per cent without anaesthetics), is wrong. Do not tell me of the advantages that accrue from these experiments. I have seen the results. Britain is a nation of invalids, not of people revelling in robust health. If it is morally wrong, then it cannot be medically right—and nothing will make it so. To cheat, to lie, to have a double standard in your business and private life is wrong. No financial or material reward can excuse one unmoral act. You must behave in your business, professional and private life according to one true code. For if it is morally wrong, it cannot be commercially right.

It is not for me to set out a rigid code of behaviour. There is not one that is applicable at all levels, anyhow. Whether you are right or not in what you do depends on your own personal degree of evolvement. It may not be wrong for a cannibal to eat his defeated enemy. This is part of his tradition. He believes he digests his enemy's strength and virtues with his body. He does not know any better. But it would be wrong for you to do this, because you *do* know better. In the same way, an ignorant man may be excused for eating the flesh of animals. But you—you know you have a trusteeship for the animal world. You know that animals are not here to be exploited, to be forced bred, to be slaughtered and eaten. If you have this knowledge and you eat meat, you are in the wrong.

If I were asked to give one simple rule for determining the rightness or wrongness of your actions, I would say STUDY YOUR MOTIVES. And in your study be true to yourself.

In your day-to-day dealings with people, your code of behaviour will invariably be right if your true motives are right.

If your motive is selfish, materialistic, and prompted by greed or lust for power, then your action will be wrong. Your life will be, to that degree, made futile and empty. The temporary gains your act may bring you will corrupt, not enrich your life. To this extent, the law of cause and effect provides its own punishment.

But when I die, you ask, will I be sent to hell and tortured by devils? Will I face a day of judgment, hear all my sins read out and have my few good deeds set against them? Will I be judged on this and, perhaps, sentenced?

No. This does not happen.

What does happen is that you sit with your spiritual helpers and review the life you have led. As it is enacted in front of you, as if on a three-dimensional television screen, so you note the mistakes you made—where you went wrong; where you were right. Every good act and every bad act is clearly seen, with the motive that prompted it and the result that followed it.

You review your life in detail. You discuss it with your guides and consider the lessons you have learned. You have then to make a decision. Are you ready to pass on to the next stage in your spiritual evolution or do you need further education at the earthly level? If you decide on the latter, you then have a long period of rest, meditation, self-appraisal and readjustment.

Then one day, refreshed, renewed and wiser, you are ready for your new course. You gather again with your guides. You review the entire process of your spiritual evolvement. A new life is chosen. Then, perhaps centuries after your first visit to this world, you sink into a deep sleep. Your spiritual memory is again temporarily erased. You enter into a fertilised seed in the womb of your new earthly mother. You have enrolled for another course in the university of life.

CHAPTER TWENTY-ONE

SUICIDES AND CHILDREN WHO DIE

WHEN you choose your life, the span of it is chosen, too. Like any other course of education, you know when it starts and when the last term ends. If you decide to end your life before its allotted span has been run, you may have to come back and live out the balance, however short. To continue the educational analogy: you may take a course but, for reasons of health, quit it before it is completed. There may be a number of lessons you missed. Your diploma is withheld. You can, if you wish, come back for another term to make up the subjects in which your instruction is incomplete.

It does not take courage to commit suicide. It is the way of the coward. It takes courage to carry on, not to give up.

Suicide decides nothing. You return to the other world and realise that the task you set yourself has not been finished. Perhaps the course was a hard one. But you chose it, and you should have stuck it out. You cannot continue your spiritual evolution until you have graduated from the present level. To do so, you need to complete the course. But you cannot reoccupy your old body. It has been buried and has rotted; or perhaps it has been burned.

You consult your guides. You decide that only a few years will enable you to gain the particular experience you now need. So you enter an earthly existence that is not destined to last long.

You know that death is neither a punishment nor a final solution. It is a step upwards. Your death certificate is a diploma in the school of life. In the same way as a student has one day to leave college and go out into the adult world, so you, too, must eventually leave this school of experience and go into the greater life.

Some spirit entities need only a short time here. This is either because they left a life unfinished or because they are mature and need little further education at this level. Often, the refined spirit who needs but a few years will choose the life of a child. Perhaps you have met one of these children. They seem wise before their years. The sweetness and purity shine through.

Those parents who suffer the loss of a child, take heart. It seems that the purity of childhood does away with some of the inhibitions adults have. Children find it much easier to communicate after they have passed over than do grown-ups. But your grief does not help. So dry your eyes. Comfort yourself that your child is near you. He is probably waiting for you to get over the parting as a prerequisite to reunion. It was James Barrie who wrote, in *Peter Pan*, "Dying would be a great adventure." And it is.

Pregnant women get odd ideas—and not always about food, although these do predominate. Jean used to get up in the middle of the night and cook an enormous fry-up. Just about the time it was ready to eat, she would feel sick and throw it all away. Expectant mothers dream and plan, to pass the waiting months. But when they get near their time, they become less concerned about whether the baby will be a boy or a girl, or if its eyes will be blue or brown, or if it will grow up tall or short, dark or fair. Most mothers will eventually settle for one characteristic—please, let my baby be normal.

Not all these prayers seem to be heard. My belief is that all our prayers are always answered. But often the answer is NO. What of the child that is born with a disability? The parents initially have a feeling of guilt. What went wrong? Were we to blame? Some parents never lose this guilt complex and their lives become an unhappy saga of remorse and over-compensation.

Birth is an amazing process. What impresses me most is not that sometimes a child is born handicapped but that hundreds of times every day babies emerge into this world perfect. Let us consider one who did not.

Some years ago, some friends of ours had a baby girl. She was their second child. The first, a boy, was a fine robust lad. The girl was physically perfect, with pale blue eyes and natural blonde hair. Yet she was incomplete: for somewhere along the line, her brain was starved of oxygen for a short while. As a result, part of her brain did not develop.

When her parents discovered that she was not responding to mental stimulus, they took her to a paediatrician. He examined the baby very thoroughly, had exhaustive tests carried out, consulted a brain specialist, and gave his verdict. The child would grow physically but not mentally. She would be literally a vegetable all her life. She should be put in a home.

This is a grave decision for any parent to have to make. Our friends asked our views. I examined the child myself. What I said came seemingly involuntarily, but I knew it originated from my guides. "Keep her," I recommended. "Show her love—lots of love. Let her receive regular spiritual healing. I cannot say how far she will develop, but she will become an intelligent personality. Keep her and love her."

Sarah is now six years old. She goes to a school for handicapped children. She is gay, lovely and loving. Her mother—who has since had another son, perfectly normal—says she seems to love Sarah best of all. Mother and daughter have established an unusual affinity. Sarah will probably never be a fully normal adult, but she is a personality in her own right.

Needing guidance in bringing up Sarah, her mother sought the help of a society for handicapped children. She found the aid she needed, but was made aware of the dearth of facilities in her own district. She is now the secretary of an active local branch of the society and has given help and advice to other parents.

Bringing up Sarah did, however, prove a strain. By the time the child was four, her mother was run down and had lost too much weight. She was painfully thin, could not keep her food down and was fast approaching a state of invalidism. Her doctors could find nothing wrong. She had innumerable tests and examinations. The results were all negative. Eventually, she was kept in hospital under observation.

Only then did her husband tell me of her plight and ask for healing. In the hospital, I found her painfully thin and gaunt. She was in her thirties, but she had the appearance of an old woman. She weighed less than a hundred pounds.

I gave her healing.

A week later, she was home. A month later, she was plump and happy, eating well and having to watch her figure. She weighed a hundred and thirty-five pounds.

There is a pattern here. I cannot see it all. Some of it remains to be woven.

In every handicapped child or disabled person resides a perfect spirit. It has chosen the life it leads. The body it occupies may be a self-made prison. The work it has chosen to do may require this. The parents, or some other persons, may need this contact. Or perhaps the life of a disabled person will provide the difficult test a spirit needs to further its evolutionary progress.

There is a design in it all. Sometimes we are too blind to see it. But it is there.

CHAPTER TWENTY-TWO

CAN I SPEAK TO MY GUIDES?

A MAN strained his elbow doing the housework while the maid was on holiday. When she came back, he found time to call on his doctor. The doctor examined him and then left him alone in the surgery, returning a few minutes later with this prescription: "Bathe your elbow three times a day in cold water." The patient thanked him and went home.

A few days later, he was back. His arm was no better. "Are you certain of the treatment you prescribed, doctor?" he asked. "My maid said I should bathe it in *hot* water."

The doctor turned a red and wrathful face on him. Full of professional dignity, he replied with emphasis, "Well, my maid said cold water!"

Ridiculous? Yes, of course it is. When you consult a doctor, you expect him to be able to deal with your problem out of his personal experience. If he has no experience of the disease you are suffering from, then you expect him to call in somebody who has—another doctor or a specialist.

The same principle applies to all professions. When you consult your solicitor, for instance, you assume he is sufficiently knowledgeable in his field to be able to advise you from a wide fund of personal experience. You are entitled to expect it, too.

If any professional man is unable to act for you and advise you because he lacks experience and has no personal knowledge of the subject on which you have consulted him, then he must say so. You are then entitled to ask him to call in a consultant. If he will not, you are justified in going elsewhere and changing your adviser. There is nothing startling or revolutionary in this. It is common sense.

Suppose the expert you consulted did not have the specialised knowledge required, and said, "I am sorry. I have no personal experience in this field. I do not even know anybody who has. But I do have some old books. These tell what people did and said on the subject many hundreds of years ago. The best I can do is to refer you to them."

Now, if a doctor, dentist, solicitor, surveyor, accountant or any other professional man made such a statement, you would probably say, "Thank you for your suggestion. But it is not good enough. I consulted you because I believed you to be an expert in this field. However, if you have no personal experience, I feel I must consult somebody who has."

This is a reasonable view. Please, then, apply the same criterion to another profession—the priesthood.

Go and see your local priest. I use the word "priest" to mean any ordained minister of religion—any minister of any orthodox religion. Explain to him the philosophical, spiritual or emotional problems you have. Tell him of your doubts about faith, your worries about life, your fear of death. See that he fully understands your need for advice from one who is spiritually and psychically qualified. Ask him what *personal* experience he has had of *solving* these problems.

Let him answer you in his own time and in his own way. When he has done so, ask yourself if the quality and factual content of his reply is adequate. Would it be adequate if he were a doctor and you had a painful and crippling disease? Would it be adequate if he were a lawyer and you were being sued for thousands of pounds you did not owe? Would it be adequate if he were a surveyor and your house was in immediate danger of collapse? No. You will be forced to admit that he does not measure up to the reasonable standards you apply to other professions.

A priest claims to be a man of God. His function is to aid those who are lacking in the psychic gifts which are necessary to attain spiritual awareness. He should listen to your problems and then be able to say, "I have dealt with many similar problems. I have communicated with the world of spirit. Calling upon their wisdom, their experience and their ability to see ahead, I have been able, positively, to ask and receive guidance. Those I have helped in this way have obtained spiritual help and guidance in their affairs. They have thus found health, harmony and tranquillity. I will communicate and ask for aid for you, too."

And when the guidance is received, he should help you to apply it. He should be your companion along the highway that has been opened out before you.

Instead, if he is an honest man, he must surely admit that he has no knowledge of the world of spirit and no ability to communicate with it. All he can do is refer you to the tales of those who could.

Priests should be clairvoyant. They should be the psychic guides of their flock. They should be clairaudient—able to hear the voices telling the way to go. They should be sensitives, full of psychic power. Then they would be able to raise their entire congregation to a higher and higher degree of spiritual awareness, so that fear, ignorance, illness and depression would be lifted and truth, knowledge and communion with God would daily take their place.

You have not previously been told the truth because your religious education was dictated by those whose power rested on your continued ignorance.

I tried to tell this to my children in simple language: for when you explain things to a child, you have to compose your thoughts carefully and use short words. When I had finished, I wrote down what I had said and it was printed in a magazine. I had a lot of letters about that piece and a great demand from parents for reprints. The article finished with this paragraph:

> I look forward to the time when all sects and religions disappear, when our intellect and our spiritual knowledge enable us all to conform to the laws of nature, and to combine religion with science for the common good of mankind.

Those of us who are in regular touch with the world of spirit do not need priests to interpret old books. Nor do you. The big advantage of psychic communication is that you can stop guessing. You can dispense with conjecture. You need not rely on what another man did or said in days gone by.

You only have to ask.

You have a spirit guide. Everybody has. You may have more

than one. Years ago, they were called guardian angels. They are evolved spirit entities who are chosen for their understanding and their experience in helping those going through life in this world. Among your guides may be a relative who was very fond of you in a previous life and who has chosen to help you in this one, or persons who passed over many centuries ago but have specialised in your present type of earthly existence. They were with you when you chose the life you are now leading. They are at hand to help you through it. And they will be the first to welcome you when it is over.

Your guides often communicate with you. Normally, they do not do so by word of mouth. Their methods of communication are limited. They will put an idea into your head, lead you to a man who will solve your problem, or help you in other ways. Eventually, as your psychic ability increases, you will become aware of the assistance they are giving you. It may prove impossible to highlight any particular act or event—that is, unless you are a sensitive.

Sensitives, or mediums, are born with the latent ability to serve as a channel for spirit communication. It is difficult for those in the other world to speak to us. To do this, they need not only to transform their level of vibration into one we can receive—as a radio does—but also to transform it again into sound waves. This requires a mechanism akin to the vocal cords of a human being. There have been examples of verbal communication where the voice was manufactured completely by the spirit people. The quickest way, though, is to use an existing piece of reproduction equipment—a human voice box.

Some mediums go into a trance. They seem to go into a deep sleep, almost a coma. This enables the guide to take over the body for a short while and talk to you. There are various depths of trance. Some sensitives seek attunement, as I do when I am healing. Some find that they are more efficient if they are in the dark, or in a room with very dim lighting. Others prefer a well lighted room or even bright daylight.

Mediumship is inherited. But like any other gift, it needs development. Some people are frightened when they find their bodies taken over by another personality. It takes time, patience, training and a great deal of personal discipline to become a

medium. A leading Spiritualist once told me that he thought his
Sometimes the medium may be fully awake, relaying messages in
whole lifetime was a training for the last ten years.

I have spoken with my guides many times. It is a habit of mine
to sit with a medium every few months. It does not matter who it
is, but I prefer someone experienced. Generally, my guides make
immediate contact—at least, those who wish to talk to me do. The
others may simply greet me and stand aside for their colleagues.
the same way as somebody who might be holding a telephone
whilst you were in the room and telling you what was being said.
At other times, the medium is in a trance and the guides talk direct
with me.

Each medium has his own guides, of course. One of these
generally acts as a "gatekeeper". His job is to control those who
wish to communicate, to see that only one at a time can do so,
and to regulate the order of things. This is an important function,
as the medium in a trance state is unable to exercise control.

A sitting usually lasts under an hour, although sometimes it goes
on much longer. The effort of communication is great, and few
spirit entities can sustain it for long. On more than one occasion I
have spoken to a spirit friend and then found that, before we had
finished our conversation, the power had started to fade and he
had to go. Perhaps two months later, I would be sitting with
another medium in another place. My friend would come through,
remind me of the previous conversation, and calmly continue it as
if we had been on the telephone, had been cut off, and had now
been reconnected. As I suppose we had.

There is, however, no such thing as "calling up spirits". It is
they who voluntarily communicate with us. All you can do is sit
with a medium from time to time and so provide spirits with the
opportunity of getting in touch with you.

As a healer, I often have to deal with sickness caused by grief.
The trappings of death are barbaric. Mourning is a form of
punishment. Self-pity, remorse and guilt are exaggerated. Those
who remain induce their own ailments.

When I heal these poor ignorant people, I try to re-educate
them towards death. A widow who has never sat with a medium—
and who has anyway choked up any channel of communication
with grief—said to me, "Why has he never got in touch with me?

If my husband survives, as you say he does, why doesn't he let me know?" She is like a sad and lonely woman who complains that nobody telephones her these days. Apart from the fact that her misery and self-pity make her a poor companion, she has not installed a telephone . . .

Remember that there is a fairly simple way for your guides to get in touch with you. It is through what I call "a quiet moment", as described on page 86.

If your guides wish to communicate, the "quiet moment" will give them the receptive conditions they need. Do not be disappointed if, after ten or fifteen minutes, nothing happens or you drop off into a light sleep. It takes practice to learn attunement. The one essential is to stop thinking about your problems. Just relax and daydream. After a few attempts, you will start to get results.

The first thing you will notice will be a lessening of your pressures. Physically and mentally, you will feel lighter. The tensions will go out of you and you will be relaxed and refreshed. The next thing you will notice is that your worries seem less important and you can think of one or two new ways of dealing with your problems.

You are getting help.

CHAPTER TWENTY-THREE

THE SILVER CORD

WHEN your life span is over and you are ready to die, you will find a great lessening of tension. You will be aware that you are nearing the end of one chapter in the book of your immortality. Since I became a spiritual healer I have helped many people to die. I now know this is an important part of a healer's duties. There may have been a history of pain and discomfort, but as the moment approaches there is peace, tranquillity, a complete absence of pain and a happy acceptance.

There are people who die on the battlefield, or in a car or plane accident. There are others who are murdered or executed. There are those, too, who have little spiritual awareness, who fight against their fate and seek no help in making this great change. For them, acceptance comes late. Often, in the spirit world, they still cannot adjust and therefore need a period of care and re-education to enable them to do so. These are the minority.

Most of the time before death is tranquil. The knowledge that the course is run, the education is finished, the trials and tribulations of this world are at an end, brings peace and acceptance. You feel a lightness. All sensations of the body seem remote and no longer part of you. You find yourself drifting upwards. You float gently like a captive balloon. You look down, and you see a body stretched out on the bed. It is yours.

Connecting this shrunken and outworn body to the real you is a thin line of silver. It pulses with a living light. This is the silver cord. As you gradually drift higher, the cord lengthens and thins out. Then the light that glows from it starts to fade, until it has gone completely and the cord can no longer be seen. At that moment, you die.

You float there for a while, looking down on the now empty

and strangely impersonal body. You are relaxed and happy. Your feeling is one of lightness—as if you are half awake after a deep refreshing sleep in which you enjoyed lovely dreams. You cannot remember any details. You cannot be bothered to do so. You are content to enjoy the dream state and to bask in the euphory of it.

In this delightful state, you drift lightly upwards through a silver-grey mist. The movement is gradual and pleasant. It is not so much upward as outward. Soon you are joined by your guides. They smile and welcome you. Together, you drift slowly through the mist. You are happy in your reunion with them and content to forget the rigours of the course you have run.

The mist thins. With your guides, you advance slowly to meet the happy, smiling crowd of relatives and friends who have preceded you. You are in the world of spirit. You are home.

The spirit people enjoy radiant bounding health and well-being. They have the appearance of the age at which they were at their best. It varies from person to person. Some men were in their prime in their forties. Some women reached their best years in the late twenties. After you die, there is an immediate dropping away of the trappings, deficiencies and appearances of old age or disease. There then starts a gradual process of change towards the age that suits you best. Your body straightens and fills out, the lines and wrinkles are smoothed away, your whole manner becomes more youthful until you reach what is the optimum condition for you. This is the form you then retain, although your face and your aura improve in beauty and light as your spiritual evolution progresses.

Children gradually grow up in the spirit world. It is a slow process and not one we can equate to our earthly concept of time. They grow up slowly whilst there are still in this world friends and close relatives who knew them as children. When they communicate—as they seem to be able to do more easily than adults—they appear as children. When their parents, and those close to them here, have been reunited with them, the process of maturing is accelerated until they, too, reach the appearance of an age that suits them best.

In an atmosphere of love and light, you renew acquaintanceships, greet old friends and enjoy the company of those you loved on earth. As time passes, you also welcome newcomers and help them to adjust to their surroundings.

Time passes. We cannot measure this time. The world is very old. Time, in our modern context, is but a pebble on a mountain, a drop of water in the ocean of eternity. But time passes. You are fully adjusted now and ready for the assessment and analysis of your last life in this world. With your guides, you reflect on it. Perhaps you are ready for the next stage of your spiritual evolution. Perhaps this stage is incomplete. You may need more experience in certain facets of life. Perhaps you lack a full measure of compassion, of humility, or of the important awareness of the need to serve others. If this is so, you decide on the new life you need to live. This time, you may inhabit the body of a cripple, a spastic child, a deaf mute, a millionaire or a genius.

CHAPTER TWENTY-FOUR

WHEN MY FATHER WENT ON AHEAD

MY father was seventy-eight when he passed on. I was standing on one side of the bed when he went. Jean was holding his hand. He sat propped up in the large double bed, a white-haired gentleman.

The illness had become apparent two weeks earlier. His doctor and two specialists confirmed that he had not long to go. They regretted there was nothing they could do.

In the beginning, he had some pain. He was given both contact and absent healing. When the time came for him to leave us, he was without pain and asleep. His passing was quiet and peaceful.

He knew his time was near. We had a long talk about it. I was proud of him. He said he had lived a good life. There was nothing more he felt he had to do. He was ready to go. He asked only that his family and friends might be spared the barbarism of a funeral. When he had finished with his body, he wanted it to be privately cremated. There was to be no mourning. He was calm and relaxed and cheerful.

My father was not a very articulate man. His education had been a simple one. He was brought up in an orthodox religion, and he did not read much. I doubt if he had ever read a book on philosophy.

He was quiet and contemplative; he smoked a pipe, and seemed to be content to observe. He was not a Spiritualist. I did try, once or twice, to interest him in it; but he seemed to feel that the same basic truths were present in all religions.

Yet without reading any books, without any theological discussion or instruction, without provocation, and with no prompting from anybody in this world, this simple and comparatively untutored man had discarded all religious orthodoxies over forty years ago.

All the religious trappings, taboos, rituals and superstitions were shed. He lived a simple life. His personal requirements could be met by a few shillings a day. He was kind, considerate and always willing to excuse the weaknesses of others. His sole philosophy was to do unto others, as he would have them do unto him.

Where did he get it from? He never displayed any psychic ability. He saw no visions, heard no voices. As far as I know, he had never visited a medium or a healer—until the last two weeks, that is—and none of his friends was a sensitive.

Somewhere along the line, he must have made contact with his guide. He may not have been aware of his expanding spiritual maturity, but it was apparent to those who knew him.

There are those of us who heal and have been healed. There are those of us who have spoken to beings in the spirit world. There are those of us who have seen them, touched them, photographed them. After these kind of demonstrations, the acceptance of the spiritual awareness and knowledge that follow is natural and unquestioned. For a man to arrive at spiritual maturity without any of these demonstrations, and with no formal introduction, needs a particular kind of purity.

A little over two hours before he went, my father passed into a light coma. At that moment, before our eyes, the life force started gradually to go from him. His spirit left his body and drifted just above him, connected by the pulsing silver cord. Gradually, the cord lengthened as the spirit moved farther away. It continued to pulse slowly.

He was looking down on us then—Jean holding his hand and I standing quietly by his bed, willing him the strength and tranquillity to aid and ease his passing.

During this time, his physical body changed. The skin of his face became sunken. The pale blue eyes were focused on infinity and looking upon eternity. The change was so great, I could no longer recognise him.

Then the silver cord stopped pulsing. It dissolved. His spirit drifted up and away . . . to be received by those he had loved who had gone before. My father was "dead".

Now he knows the things he believed are true. And he will prepare a place for us when it is our time to join him.

Next day, I picked up a copy of *The Bewildered Man's Guide to Death* and read what I had written there. It is a slim booklet and does not take long to read. As I put it down, Jean said, "Would you wish, now, to change anything?"

No. It is all there. In these pages I have enlarged on some of the things I wrote then, and I have filled in some details. The facts are the same.

When I was young, I regarded my father as a "bewildered man". But then I believe his guide got through to him and gave him the ability of knowing.

My father has since communicated with me. I have needed his help. After a period of adjustment, he is now managing to get through to me. The help and advice is, as it always was, gentle and touched with the purity of goodness and truth. I try hard to follow this path. When we are again reunited, I do so want him to be proud of me.

CHAPTER TWENTY-FIVE

SHALL I STILL BE MARRIED
IN THE NEXT WORLD?

THERE is no lust, sex or bodily love in the next world. Although you might have enjoyed these sensual pleasures, they are primitive. There, you will rise above this level of pleasure. Do not feel deprived. There are compensations and levels of pleasure and happiness undreamed of here. But since sensual emotions are discarded with other earthly characteristics, whether you remain married or not is probably less important.

There are some marriages here that are founded on love. I do not mean sexual compatibility, since this is only one type of the physical demonstration of love. I mean where there is a true spiritual affinity.

If your marriage was founded on a love so great as to amount to a spiritual affinity, then—and only then—it will survive. When one partner passes over, the period until the other follows will see the spiritual partner watching over the temporal one. When they are eventually reunited, they will live together in the next world in perfect harmony and understanding. They will pass on to the next stage of their spiritual evolution together and will not again be parted. But this applies only to those marriages founded on a true spiritual love. Love, and love alone, is the criterion.

It matters not one whit whether you were married in a church, a synagogue, a mosque or a registrar's office. The superstitions, rituals and taboos of orthodox religions mean nothing. The blessings of priests or rabbis, the prayers and the oaths, have no effect. A man and woman married in a fine cathedral have no greater call on continued happiness than those married by a crude tribal ceremony in the rain-forests of the Amazon. If between the two of you there exists a love so powerful as to amount to an affinity, you

K

are bound together in one combined spiritual entity. Your marriage will have achieved the union of two souls and it will survive death.

If your marriage has not reached this level, then it cannot continue. In the next world, you may be good friends and you may be together during the period of adjustment. But eventually you will part, and you will live independent lives.

This test is a simple one to apply. When you two are reunited after death, you will know if the affinity level was reached. You will know, because in the next world there are no lies, no pretences, no inhibitions. You are true to yourself, and you will know. You may have been married more than once. It is of no account. Only with one person in your earthly existence could you have achieved a mutual love of such a high order. Only once in a lifetime could you know this affinity. You will be reunited only with the partner with whom you achieved it.

CHAPTER TWENTY-SIX

ARE FUNERALS REALLY NECESSARY?

THE rites and taboos surrounding the death of the human body are diverse and fascinating.

The Karens, for instance, will tie their children to part of the house when a funeral goes by. This is to prevent the souls of the children leaving them to enter into the passing corpse. But they must use a special kind of string and the child must be tethered to one particular corner of the house.

The people of the Loyalty Islands believe the dead can steal the souls of the living. When a man is near death, the people go to the burial place and start whistling. This they keep up in procession to the sick man's house. They feel that if his spirit has been lured away they can just as well lure it back.

In China, when the lid of a coffin is to be closed the bystanders retreat a few steps. Some even go into another room. They believe that if their shadow is enclosed in the coffin, they, too, will die. The undertaker will only stand on the side of the grave away from the sun; and the gravediggers and coffin-bearers keep their shadows firmly attached to their persons by tying them with a special piece of cloth around their waists.

In the Bering Strait, the Esquimaux stop all work on the day a person dies. The relatives do not work for three days. During this period, they must not use a knife or any other sharp instrument for fear of hurting the departing spirit. Nor must they make any loud noise, in case they frighten it.

As far away as Roumania, a similar taboo is applied. No one will use a sharp knife, or even leave it with the edge exposed, after a death.

The Chinese also have this fear and will not even use chopsticks. For seven days after a death, all food is eaten with the fingers.

On the third, sixth, ninth and fortieth day after a death, the Lithuanians prepare a meal. They stand at their door and invite the spirit to eat and drink. Then they ask it to go away as it has now eaten and drunk its fill. The Prussians practise a similar ritual.

In Southern India, the Badagas have a ritual of transferring the sins of the deceased to a buffalo calf. The head of the tribe, or an elder, stands by the head of the corpse and recites all the sins the dead man might have committed. The dead man's hand is then placed on the calf and his sins are transferred to the animal. The little buffalo is then driven far from the village and kept isolated. For the rest of its natural life, it will be unmolested and regarded as a sacred animal.

The Egyptians had very complicated funeral rites. They believed in the resurrection. But it was the resurrection of Osiris. This, they reasoned, was a promise of their own survival of death. If, on his death, a man's friends did for him what the gods had done for Osiris, then he too would enjoy everlasting life. Therefore, the Egyptian funeral rites were a replica of what Anubis, Horus and the rest performed over the dead god. It was a long ceremony, including a complete re-enactment of the time when Osiris died and his relatives and friends wove strange spells to convert his broken body into the first mummy. In thousands of tombs opened in the Nile valley are recorded the mysteries of the resurrection. Those, as can now be demonstrated, were performed for every dead Egyptian. As Osiris rose from the dead, so all men hoped to rise and so enjoy life eternal.

I have in front of me, as I write, *The Book of Common Prayer*. In it is the service for funerals. I suggest you read it. This book is available at any library or large bookshop. It is probably the most unread book in the country. Open it at "The Order for the Burial of the Dead". It starts with a note for the priest. He is told that these prayers are "not to be used for any that die unbaptized, or excommunicate, or have laid violent hands upon themselves". The service is too long to reproduce in full here, but you should get hold of a copy and read it. The general meaning I am sure you know. The soul is put to rest until the great resurrection day when, through the meditation of Jesus, the deceased could be qualified to live for ever. Here are a few extracts:

We leave him in God's hands till the great resurrection day when body and soul will be reunited . . .

We shall not sleep, but we shall all be changed in a moment, in the twinkling of an eye, at the last trump, for the trumpet shall sound and the dead shall be raised incorruptible, and we shall all be changed . . .

And that in the general resurrection in the last day we may be found acceptance in Thy sight . . .

O holy and most merciful Saviour, deliver us not into the bitter pains of eternal death . . .

We give thee hearty thanks, for that it hath pleased thee to deliver this our brother out of the miseries of this sinful world; beseeching thee, of thy gracious goodness, shortly to accomplish the number of thine elect, and to hasten thy Kingdom; that we, with all those that are departed in the true faith of thy holy name, may have our perfect consummation and bliss, both in body and in soul, in thy eternal and everlasting glory.

The usual service has a few hymns in a similar vein. The prayers and the hymns are couched in the old language priests employ, but the basic messages are clear. They fall into two categories. The first is a general pleading for the dead person. It is a sort of spiritual character reference, with the plea that he was really not a bad chap and should seriously be considered as "one of us"—"one of us" being those that are favoured and get the bonus of eternal life. The other message is more direct. It simply tells God what to do.

The service is designed to make sure that the dear departed is clearly recognised, on the day of resurrection, as one of the elect. He will be all right. The service was in accordance with the regulations. A mark has been made against his name in the big book.

If you are not a member of the church—that is to say, if you have not been baptised into it—or if you were a member but have been thrown out (excommunicated), you do not qualify for this service. Nor do you if you are a suicide. Nor do you if you are a member of some other orthodox religion. It is only the select few who get this chance of immortality.

Now, all this is quite untrue. It is based on fear and superstition. You can no more ensure eternal life by being baptised into the church and buried by it than you can get rid of your sins into the body of a live buffalo.

There is a refreshing wind of change that is sweeping away these old superstitions. Few today believe in eternal damnation. The more enlightened churchgoers are turning towards spiritual awareness as the criterion of maturity. Soon, I hope, there will come a time when superstition is replaced by reason, fear by love, and the true message that Jesus preached will be allowed to be understood in all its superb simplicity.

When a body dies, the only intelligent thing to do is call in an undertaker. To him you say, "This person has now put aside his earthly body. It served him well. Please take it away and, without ceremony, have it burnt." Then gather together his friends and relations. Have a simple party, if you like. Let people pay their respects and say not "goodbye" but "au revoir". Have present, if you can, a medium or clairvoyant. He may, perhaps, be able to interpret some of the joys at the reception the "dead" one receives. There should be no mourning, no black. You have come to see someone off on a journey to an exciting new life. When he gets there and has settled in, perhaps he will get in touch with you and tell you all about it. You now have the knowledge that negates ignorant speculation.

Be honest. What affords you the greatest comfort—the burial service and barbaric funeral trappings of orthodox superstition, or the simplicity that truth and knowledge brings?

Some time ago, I read a poem. I do not know who wrote it and I have been unable to trace its origins. I was so impressed with the truth of it that I wrote it down:

As the faint dawn crept upwards, grey, grey and dim,
He saw her move across the past to him—
Her eyes as they had looked in long-gone years,
Tender with love, and soft with thoughts of tears,
Her hands, outstretched as if in wonderment,

Nestled in his, and rested there, content.
"Dear wife," he whispered, "what glad dream is this?
I feel your clasp—your long remembered kiss
Touches my lips, as when you used to creep
Into my heart; and yet, this is not sleep—
Is it some vision, that with night will fly?"
"Nay, dear," she answered; "it is really I."
"Dear heart, it is you I know,
But I knew not the dead could meet us so.
Bodied as we are—see, how like we stand!"
"Like," she replied, "in form, and face, and hand."
Silent awhile, he held her to his breast,
As if afraid to try the further test—
Then speaking quickly, "Must you go away?"
"Husband," she murmured, "neither night nor day!"
Close to her then she drew his head,
Trembling, "I do not understand," he said.
"I thought the spirit world was far apart . . ."
"Nay," she replied, "it is not now, dear heart!
Quick, hold fast my hand, lean on me . . . so . . .
Cling to me, dear, 'tis but a step to go!"
The white-faced watchers rose beside the bed;
"Shut out the day," they sighed. "Our friend is dead."

CHAPTER TWENTY-SEVEN

SUPPOSE YOU WERE GOING
TO DIE TONIGHT?

I SPENT an hour not long ago with a young man who had cancer. He knew the details of the disease and that his doctors had given him only two months to live. I explained to him that there were only two courses open. Either he would be healed or he would not. If he was not healed, then he had time to prepare himself for a great adventure. In either event, after two months he would no longer have a diseased body.

What would you do if you knew you had not long to live? Suppose you were going to die tonight...

The materials preparations are simple enough. You check that your will is in order. You see that your affairs are properly documented; that your assets are recorded; that your dependants are cared for, as far as you are able; and that enough information has been left for your executors to carry out your wishes. If you are poor and have no possessions, then you are spared these petty formalities.

The spiritual preparations are not so easy. Dying is a great adventure. You are going to make a journey from this world to the next. How do you plan the trip?

Suppose, in an age of space travel, you were planning a journey to Mars. The first thing you would do would be to find out all you could about Mars. You would get books out of the library. You would read guide-books, look at pictures, study reports on conditions there. You would seek out people who had been there. "What's it really like?" you would ask.

But if you knew that to return to your present life here was not possible, you would be doubly industrious in your research. And if you were told that on arrival you became a Martian, you would want to know a lot about the Martians, too.

All of us are going to undertake a journey that makes a visit to Mars look like a day trip to the sea. And the journey to the next world needs preparation, like any other major step. The preparation for this great change we call death is called "life". The study of the route is called "Spiritualism". There are guide-books for the route and for the journey. Many who have gone have come back for a while to tell us how to prepare, how to travel, what it is like there, and what happens to all travellers.

The one thing you cannot ascertain is when you will go. The duration of your life in this world is known, but not to you. You may live to be a hundred. You may be run down by a bus this afternoon. You cannot know when the great adventure will begin.

There is, therefore, only one proper course to adopt. You must be prepared to start at any time. You must live each day as though it is your last.

The past is finished. Nothing you can now do can change one minute incident. You did and said foolish things; you made mistakes; you erred. You cannot change one past action. You can only benefit from the lessons you have learned. Do not waste your time or drain your emotions with remorse or regret. Remember only the moral, not the tragedy. Any fool can benefit from his successes. But you are not a fool. You are going to benefit from your failures. The past has taught you a lot. It has added to your moral and spiritual stature; it has shown you mistakes; it has demonstrated the natural law of cause and effect. Be grateful for the past. Without it, you would not be the person you are. It was the mistakes and misfortunes that shaped you, as well as the good things and the happiness. Forget the past. But remember well what it taught you.

The future is not here yet. You cannot know what it will bring. You do not know if there will be any tomorrow. Nothing you can do can inhibit the future. It is the great unknown; the wonderful challenge of adventure; the thrill of the bend in the road; the top of the hill you have not yet crested. What lies ahead, you cannot tell. You do not want to know. The great exciting future is like the next course of a banquet; the next act of a play; the next episode of a gripping adventure. All you can do is be ready for it.

The present *is* here. Today is today. You have crested one hill and the view is fantastic. Ahead, the road winds and is lost in mist.

Today, the sun shines; the adventure is here and you are slap-bang in the middle of it. Live today to the full. There is only one philosophy: TRUST GOD AND LIVE ONE DAY AT A TIME. Live today. Do your very best with it. Enjoy yourself. Apply the lesson the past has taught you.

When the day is finished, lay it gratefully aside. Thank God for this day which is now over. It was unique. There will never be another exactly like this one. Tomorrow is not yet born. Sleep. Tomorrow may never come. Your life here may be ended tonight. You cannot know. All you do know is that you must "die" some time. Therefore, live your life as if every day is your last. Savour the sights, the sounds, the smells, the love, the laughter and the wonderful variety of it all. Act always so that you can leave this life at any time without remorse.

Once you have your life here in its proper perspective, the futility of the frustration, material acquisitiveness, lust, envy, covetousness and unhappiness that colour your mind and poison your body can clearly be seen. Divorce them from this day. Replace them with tranquillity, love, compassion, understanding, tolerance and laughter.

As a healer, I know that the full realisation of your immortality is a panacea. This is a treatment that heals all ailments. It prevents them, too. If these words could be read by everybody and immediately put into effect, the hospitals would be empty, the doctors would have leisure time in plenty, and the economic problems of the Western world would be solved.

This is only the kindergarten of your spiritual education. Make it as happy and as spiritually rewarding as you can.

Your journey to maturity may begin tonight.